PRACTICAL PLANNING ENGINEERING

About The Book –

This book has been entirely devoted to civil engineers and construction engineers who work in planning. Planning is the most important component of the process of building. The main reason for writing this book is that no one wants to share their knowledge with others anymore, which limits their ability to earn a living. By taking full responsibility for explaining the duties of a planning engineer in this book, I hope to assist any engineer in becoming a better planning engineer. I hope that by doing so, I may assist everyone in improving their work and a better planning engineer.

About The Author

Rahul (Nitin) Gupta was born in Bansgaon Post Ugharpur Sultanpur, Uttar Pradesh, India on January 12, 1992. His grandpa "Ram Anjor Gupta" and father "Ram Achal Gupta" were both businessmen, and his mother Neelam Gupta was a housewife. Rahul is now working as a Planning Lead after completing Civil Engineering, BE Civil, and a professional Certification Course of Civil Works (Billing Engineering, Tendering & Procurement Management, and Project Management). He has worked in several parts of India and is now working in Canada. Along with the job, he did not cease working and studying, which is crucial.

Rahul has seen While working, it was seen that people do not wish to help anyone, which prevents people from developing their skills. As a result, people have a lot of difficulties doing their jobs, so Rahul decided to write a good book based on our practical experience so that people can get knowledge as well as skill development and people's work can be done well and people can do their job well and they move forward.

NO	Category	Page Number
1	**Construction – Schedule Preparation**	
2	**Schedule update check list**	
3	**Schedule Updating Procedure**	
4	**Weekly report Check List**	
5	**Work Loaded Schedule updates**	
6	**Performance Evaluation**	
7	**Project Scope and Objectives (Project Tracking on MSP)**	
8	**Identify all the tasks required to complete the project**	
9	**Determine Task Dependencies**	
10	**Estimate Task Durations**	
12	**Assign Resources**	
13	**Load Resources**	
14	**Define Task Constraints and Deadlines**	
15	**Set Baseline**	
16	**Track Progress and Update Schedule**	
17	**Adjust the Schedule**	
18	**Communicate Schedule Updates**	

37	**Project Controlling & Management**	
38	**Project Management**	
39	**Project Change Management**	
40	**Project Management Interview Questions and Answers**	
41	**Prolongation Cost Claim**	
42	**Rate analysis**	
43	**Estimation**	
44	**About the FIDIC**	
45	**Schedule Narrative report**	
46	**Manpower Productivity**	

How we can Prepare New Schedule – (Construction – Schedule Preparation)

Introduction-: Creating a project schedule in Microsoft Project, although daunting, is rather simple once you understand this project management software. Generally speaking, it's the core part of any Microsoft Project Training course.

In order to ensure MS Project behaves the way you want it to, it is important to set some options prior to creating your project plan.

The first setting we will make is to specify **Auto Scheduled** mode. Be sure to have a project open in order to perform this step.

1. Specify Auto-Scheduled mode

- Navigate **File** > **Options**
- Select the **Schedule** Page
- Locate in the **Schedule options for this project** section and select **Auto Scheduled** for **New tasks created**.

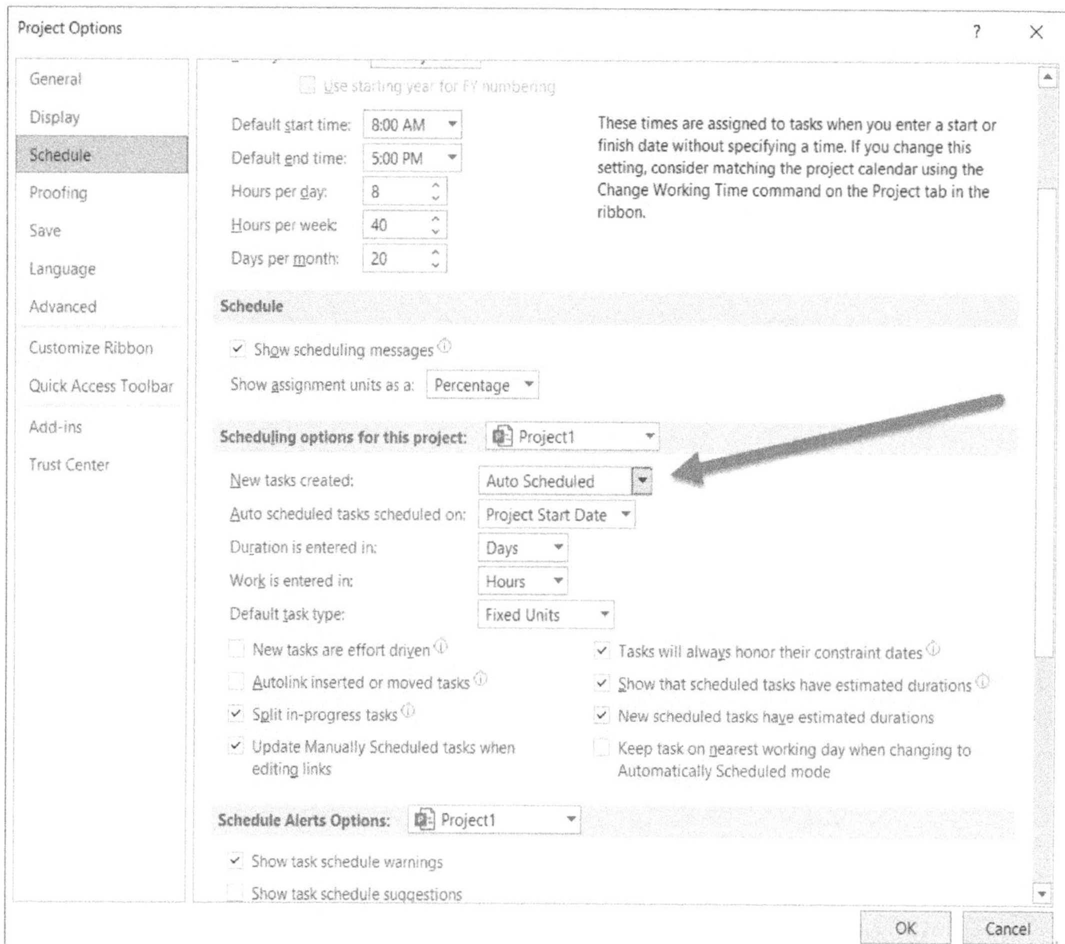

1. **Why use auto Scheduled mode?**

What this setting does is it ensures the tasks in your project will be scheduled (Start, End) based on their relationships to other tasks, as well as the assigned resources working days in relation to the project calendar selected. This is what we want in order to have our schedule reflect reality. If the tasks did not automatically schedule we could just use a tool like Excel and type in a bunch of static tasks.

It is the scheduling of Microsoft Project that makes the software such a powerful project management tool.

Go ahead and close the Project Options dialog box. You will now notice in the bottom left of the view that New Tasks : Auto Scheduled.

2. **Calculate Project after each edit**
   - Locate the setting Calculate project after each edit setting in the
   Calculation section and turn it on.

This setting tells Microsoft Project to re-calculate the project schedule immediately after every change we make to it. Meaning, when we change Work we want to timeline/critical path to be immediately updated in order to understand the impact of the change. This is important because as project managers we need to always have our information up-to-date.

Calculation

Calculate project after each edit:

◉ On

○ Off

3- Open a Blank Project

- From within MS Project navigate File > New, then select the Blank project option.

We should now have a blank Gantt Chart view as shown below:

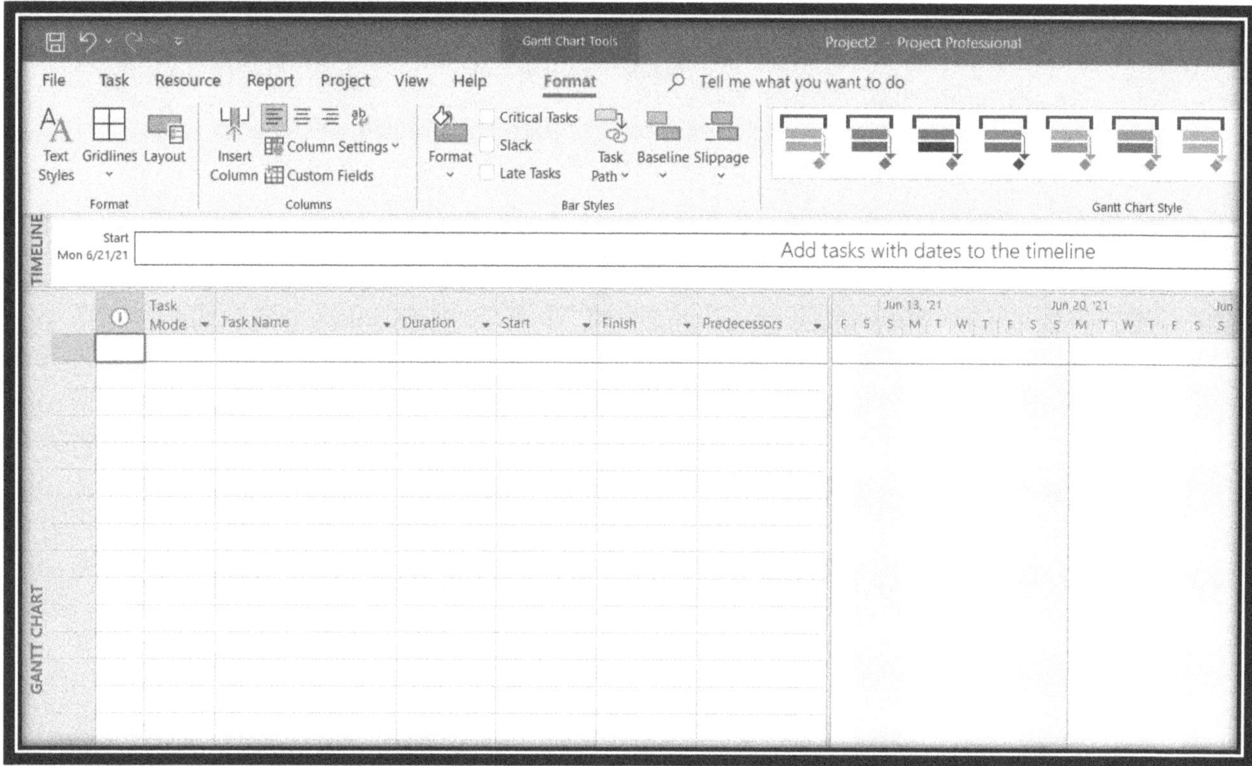

4- Insert the Project Summary Task

Now that we have our blank Gantt Chart ready for tasks we are going to display the Project Summary Task. This task will contain all other tasks in the project and is a big help to see the aggregate numbers.

- Navigate to the Format ribbon and in the Show/Hide section select the checkbox for Project Summary Task.

You should now see something like that shown below. Once we save the project, Project2 shown below will reflect the project name.

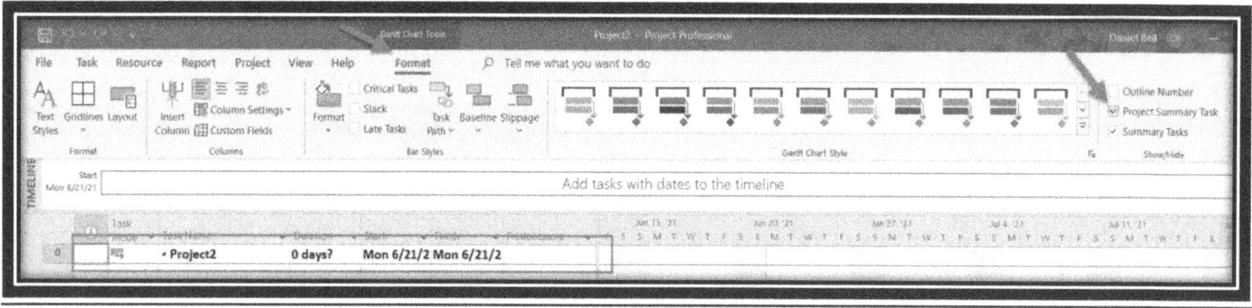

5- Save The Project

- Navigate File > Save As , select the folder you want to save the project in.
- Now give your project a name in the Save As dialog box, then click the Save button.

Set the Project Start Date

Another important step is to tell Microsoft Project when you project starts. Even if you don't know the exact date, enter one as close to when you think the project may start.

- Navigate: On the Project tab in the Properties section click the Project Information button.
- In the Project Information for New Business dialog select a Start Date. In our example I selected 6/21/2021.

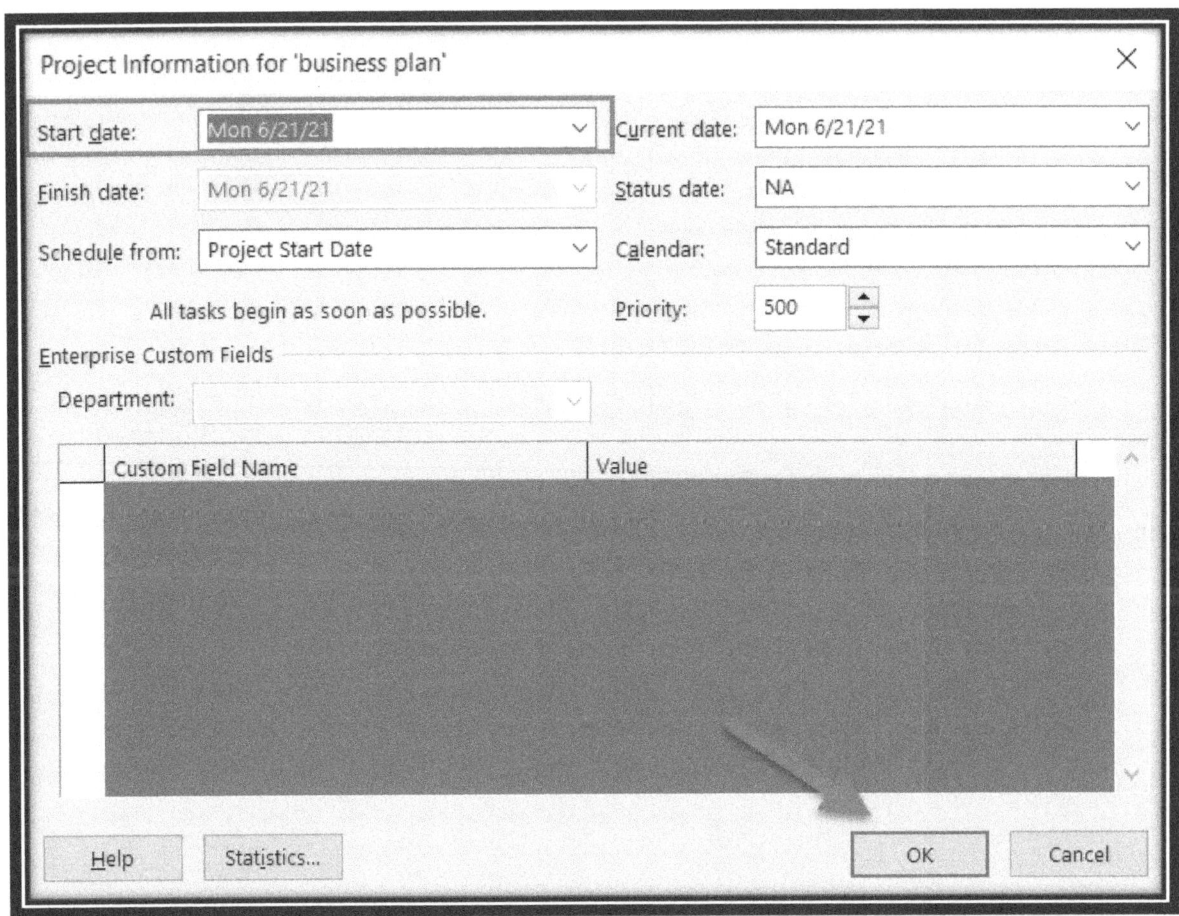

1. There are several other items to note in this dialog box.
   - Status Date: displays a vertical line in the Gantt Chart to reflect the selected Status Date. This is commonly used when creating a Status Report
   - Schedule from: This setting tells project whether to schedule the tasks based on a Start Date or an End Date. Although it may be tempting to have Project when you should start your project based on a given End Date, it is always recommended to schedule from the Start Date.

2. Enter your Work Breakdown Structure (Task List)

- Let's go ahead and enter the Tasks into Microsoft Project. I typically use the Gantt Chart view to create my WBS.

Below is what the Gantt looks like after entering the task list. Go ahead and enter the tasks shown in the screenshot below:

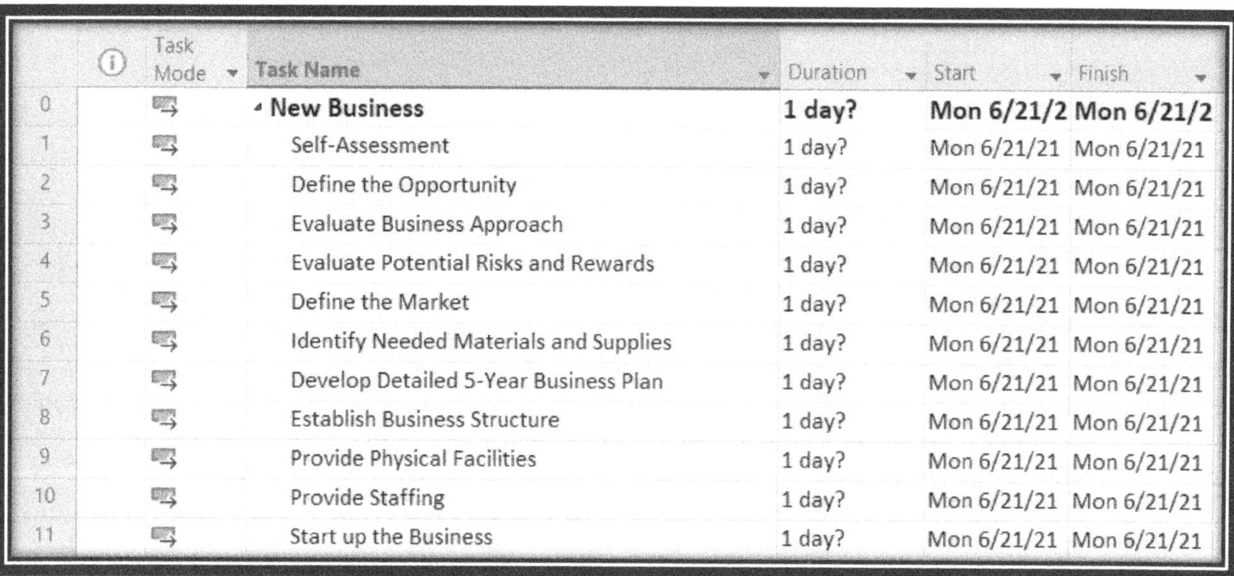

(i)	Task Mode	Task Name	Duration	Start	Finish
0		◢ **New Business**	**1 day?**	**Mon 6/21/2**	**Mon 6/21/2**
1		Self-Assessment	1 day?	Mon 6/21/21	Mon 6/21/21
2		Define the Opportunity	1 day?	Mon 6/21/21	Mon 6/21/21
3		Evaluate Business Approach	1 day?	Mon 6/21/21	Mon 6/21/21
4		Evaluate Potential Risks and Rewards	1 day?	Mon 6/21/21	Mon 6/21/21
5		Define the Market	1 day?	Mon 6/21/21	Mon 6/21/21
6		Identify Needed Materials and Supplies	1 day?	Mon 6/21/21	Mon 6/21/21
7		Develop Detailed 5-Year Business Plan	1 day?	Mon 6/21/21	Mon 6/21/21
8		Establish Business Structure	1 day?	Mon 6/21/21	Mon 6/21/21
9		Provide Physical Facilities	1 day?	Mon 6/21/21	Mon 6/21/21
10		Provide Staffing	1 day?	Mon 6/21/21	Mon 6/21/21
11		Start up the Business	1 day?	Mon 6/21/21	Mon 6/21/21

1. If you look closely at the task list you realize the we have not given MS Project the information it needs to create a critical path. Project needs to know either the Work or Duration, as well as the dependencies between the tasks. Once we start entering this information the timeline will be calculated.
2. Enter Task Durations

First we will tell MS Project how long we think the tasks of the project will take to complete. We could provide the amount of Work each task will require to be completed, and based on the assigned resource MS Project would calculate the Duration. In this case, however, we want keep our project simple.

Keep in mind that Duration is the amount of time it will take to complete a task.

Work on the other hand is where we specify the Effort required to complete a task.

- Using the Duration column, lets enter durations for the tasks of our project. We can use a "d" or "w" to specify increments of time (as well as others).

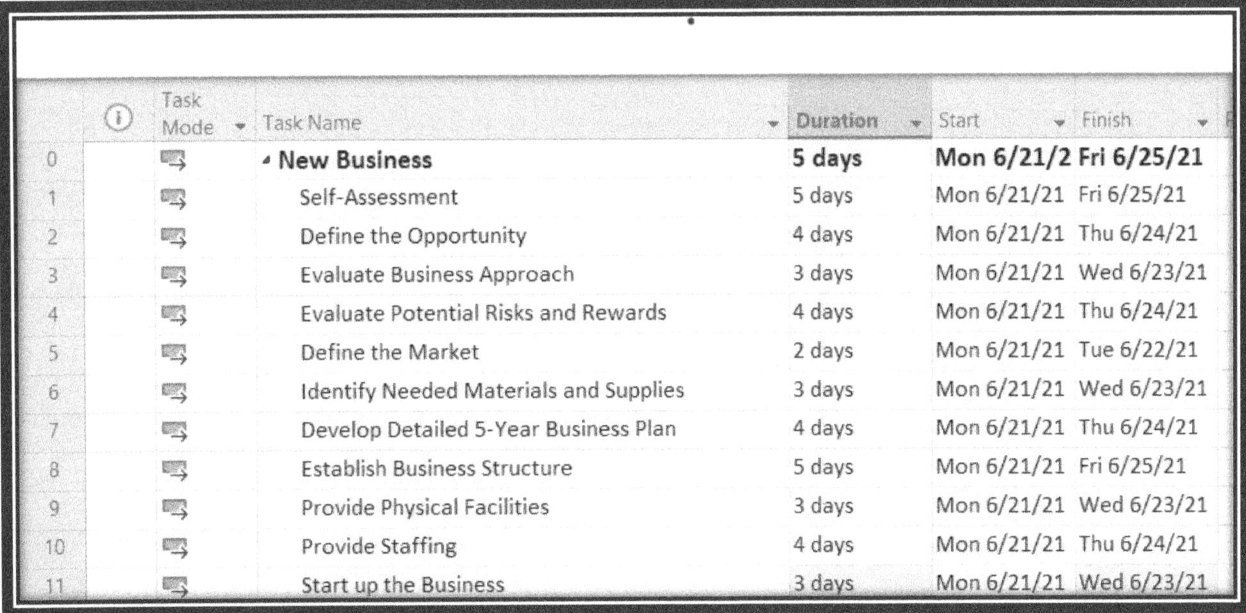

6- Create Task Dependencies: Predecessor Column

If you recall we stated the tasks need to be completed in a specific order. This is where Task Dependencies (or linking tasks) comes into play. We can create dependencies one of several ways.
• Specify task ID in predecessor / successor column
• Click and connect Gantt Bars in the Gantt Chart.
• Select two or more tasks and click the Link the selected tasks button on the Task ribbon

Let's look at this process starting with the first two tasks:
• Self-Assessment
• Define the Opportunity

In this case we want to complete the Self-Assessment prior to starting work on defining the opportunity. Certainly, some of our tasks may be able to have overlap, however, we're going to use a waterfall approach for all of them.

In order to tell Microsoft Project Define the Opportunity comes after Self-Assessment, we enter the ID of the task Self-Assessment in the Predecessor column of Define the Opportunity. This is because one task must preceded the other.

- Therefore do as follows: enter a 1 (the ID of Self-Assessment) in the Predecessor column of Define the Opportunity.

If you now look at the Gantt Chart, you will see the Self-Assessment must be completed before Define the Opportunity. The Start and End dates also reflect that the two tasks happen sequentially. The relationship used in this particular case is called a Finish to Start relationship.

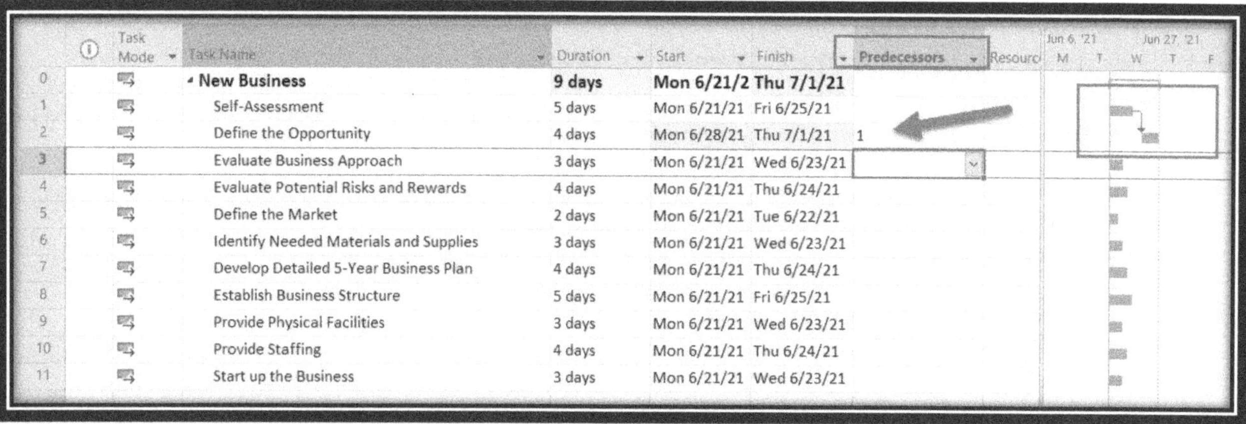

1. If you look closely you will also notice that although Self-Assessment finishes on 6/25, Define the Opportunity does not start until 6/28, which is 2 days later. This is because MS Project skipped the weekend as our Project Calendar is a 5-day work-week calendar with weekends for no work.
2. Create Task Dependencies: Link Task Button

   - Select the task Define The Opportunity, hold the ctrl key, and select Evaluate Business Approach.
   - With both tasks selected, click the Link the Selected Tasks button on the Tasks ribbon.

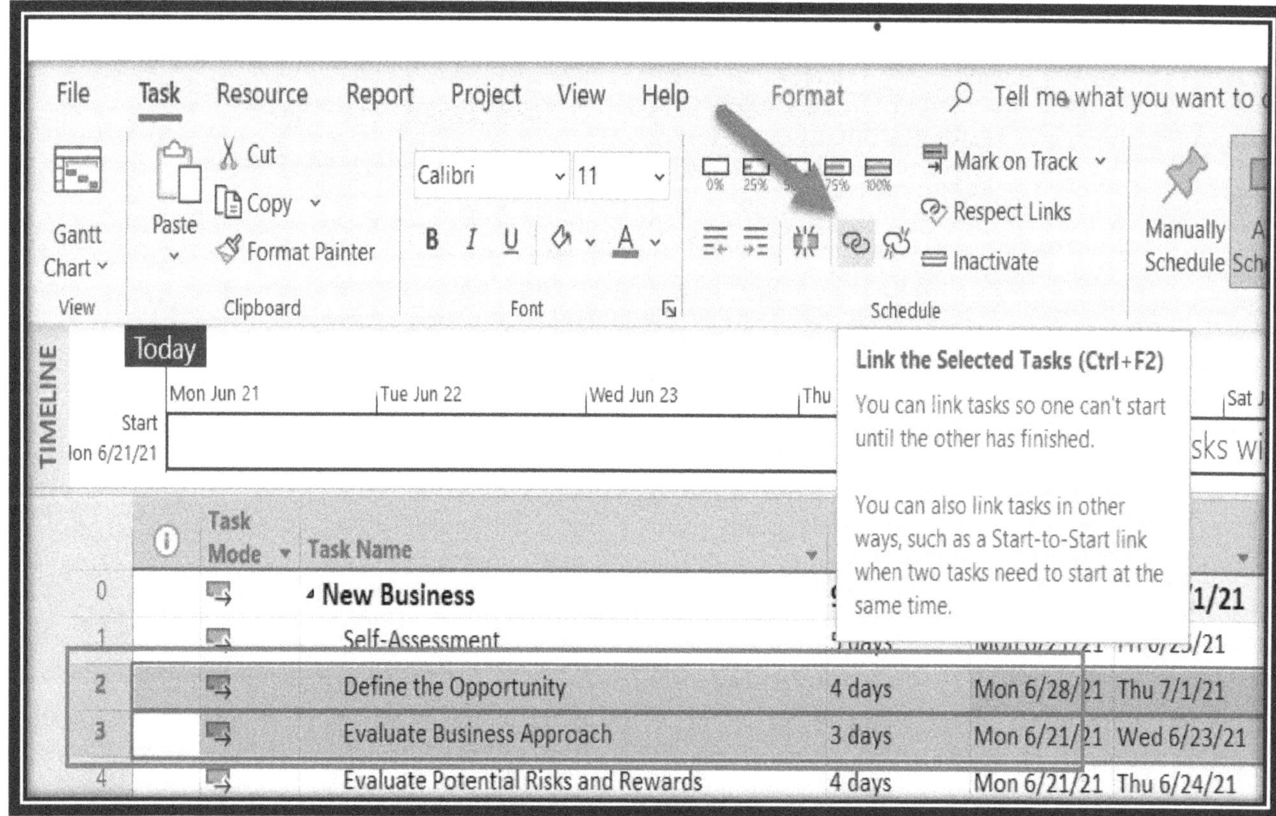

1. Now noticed that we also have a Finish to Start relationship between Define the Opportunity and Evaluate Business Approach
2. Create Task Dependencies: Remaining Tasks

    Now lets to ahead and link all the remaining tasks of the project.
    - Select the task Evaluate Business Approach, then hold the Shift key and select the last task Start up the Business.

    You should now have those two tasks and all tasks in between selected.

    - Go ahead and click the Link Selected Tasks button in the Task ribbon.

    All your tasks should now be linked and your Gantt Chart should reflect the entire timeline of your project as shown below:

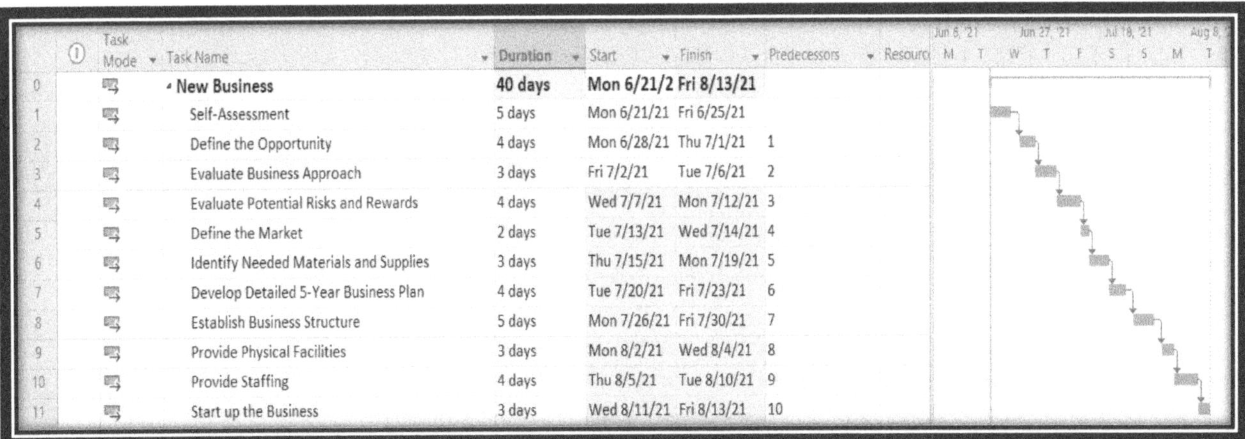

	Task Mode	Task Name	Duration	Start	Finish	Predecessors	Resource
0		⊿ New Business	40 days	Mon 6/21/2	Fri 8/13/21		
1		Self-Assessment	5 days	Mon 6/21/21	Fri 6/25/21		
2		Define the Opportunity	4 days	Mon 6/28/21	Thu 7/1/21	1	
3		Evaluate Business Approach	3 days	Fri 7/2/21	Tue 7/6/21	2	
4		Evaluate Potential Risks and Rewards	4 days	Wed 7/7/21	Mon 7/12/21	3	
5		Define the Market	2 days	Tue 7/13/21	Wed 7/14/21	4	
6		Identify Needed Materials and Supplies	3 days	Thu 7/15/21	Mon 7/19/21	5	
7		Develop Detailed 5-Year Business Plan	4 days	Tue 7/20/21	Fri 7/23/21	6	
8		Establish Business Structure	5 days	Mon 7/26/21	Fri 7/30/21	7	
9		Provide Physical Facilities	3 days	Mon 8/2/21	Wed 8/4/21	8	
10		Provide Staffing	4 days	Thu 8/5/21	Tue 8/10/21	9	
11		Start up the Business	3 days	Wed 8/11/21	Fri 8/13/21	10	

7- Create Milestones

Milestones are an important part of your project schedule. Most often they will represent the completion of a specific set of tasks that produce a deliverable. Or perhaps a significant event in your project. Nonetheless, they are something you and the entire project team are working toward in an effort to complete the project. In our case we are going to create one simple milestone noting the creation of our business.

The way we do this is by entering one more task at the very end of the project named.

- Enter a task named Business Complete, and specify a Duration of 0 days.

Specifying a Duration of 0 turns the task into a Milestone.

- Finally we create a relationship between the task we just created and the task before it, Start Up The Business.

Use one of the previously described methods to create that relationship. When complete your schedule should look like the one below:

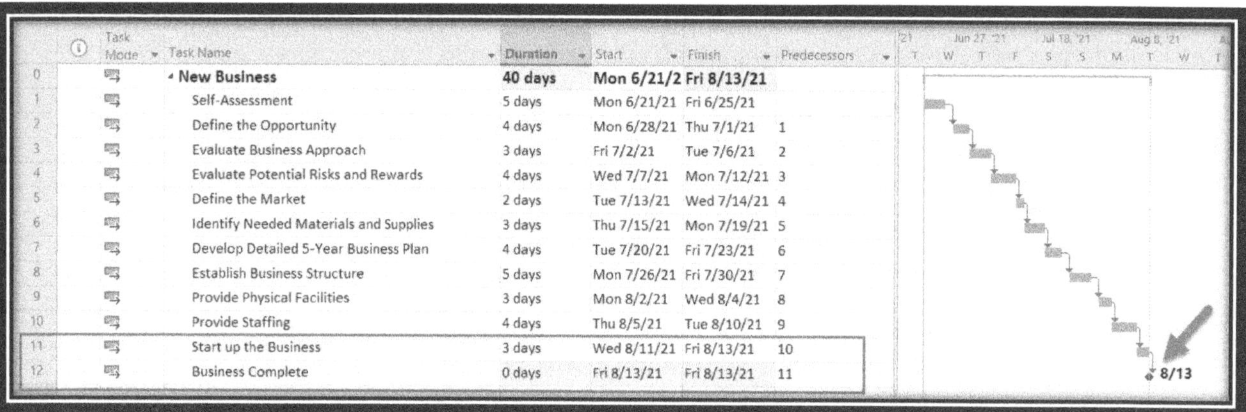

Schedule Update Check List

Sl. No	Description	Check box
1.	Project Start Date to be checked for its correctness	
2.	Project End Date shall not change. If we change there should be a justification to the same. The changes has to be mentioned / highlighted in the report.	
3.	Check the Task % Complete for all activities if it is updated correctly.	
4.	Task Constraints (There shall not be any constrains as project will not update properly if there are constrains in the successor activities)	
5.	Check "Task Baseline Start Date Variance" after the update of the schedule. If there are any variance, we need to check if the update is correct. If the update is correct, we need to check the reason for variance and have a justification for the change.	
6.	Check "Task Baseline Finish Date Variance" after the update of the schedule. If there are any variance, we need to check if the update is correct. If the update is correct, we need to check the reason for variance and have a justification for the change.	
7.	Task Notes shall be maintained to keep record of issues, problems happening in that activity.	
8.	Critical Path After updating the schedule check for the critical path every time if the Tasks are same as previous update or critical path has changed. If the critical path has changed then we need to have a justification for the change and needs to be highlighted to client.	
9.	Task Deadlines as per agreement with client to be fixed (To check the slippage in the WBS) if there are any changes, then we need to have proper justification for the change.	
10.	Task Relationships (Lag, Lead) No negative lag is to be provided in any relationship	

	FS + Lag should not be given. If this needs to be given then that lag duration has to be converted to an activity. SF relationship should not be used in any schedule. SS+Lag , FF + lag can be provided.	
11.	Work Variance after the schedule is updated, it should be Zero. If there are any changes, then it needs to be rectified.	
12.	Actual Start and Actual Finish Dates shall not contain Future dates (>Status Date)	
13.	No start or Finish activities without actual dates that are < Status Date. (If any dates are not achieved then change the relationship and provide lags if required)	
14.	<u>Activities which are having FS relationship:</u> No Successors shall be updated with Actual Start date without updating predecessor. (If any successor Task have started before the finish of its predecessor, then change the relationship of that activity to SS + lag to avoid the scheduling conflict).	
15.	After completing the update, check for any Scheduling conflict error. If there are any, then it needs to be checked and rectified.	
16.	While updating the actuals check if the duration of the activity is greater than or Equal to one day unless the Task is milestone else the weightage of the physical/actual progress will not be recorded in the WBS level even though the Task progress is 100%. To update an activity with duration of one day, we need to provide the actual start date only. After the percentage complete needs to be updated to 100%. Then the progress will be correctly reflected in the WBS level progress.	
17.	If any of the activity has started and was not complete in time due to reasons like work has stopped, to maintain the weightage of such activities use the split activity option which will maintain the same duration assigned to activity by forecast date of such activities and be changed to the future date else project progress will keep on changing even after there is no physical/actual progress achieved.	
18.	Schedule Update project function is to be run after all the activities in the schedule has been updated. When is function is run, the system should not show any error. If there are any, then it needs to be rectified till the schedule has been updated with out any error.	
19.	Set the page layout, paper size and timeline of the schedule on each week update before converting into PDF	

Procedure for Updating the Schedule

Step 1: Establish a Baseline Schedule

1. Create a new project in Microsoft Project.
2. Define project tasks, durations, and dependencies using the Gantt Chart view.
3. Assign resources to each task.
4. Set the baseline by going to the Project menu, selecting Set Baseline, and choosing Baseline or Baseline 1.

Step 2: Update Task Status

1. Open the project file in Microsoft Project.
2. Navigate to the Task Sheet view by clicking on the View tab and selecting Task Sheet.
3. Update task progress by entering actual start dates in the "Actual Start" column.
4. Adjusting remaining durations for tasks based on the progress made.
5. Specifying the appropriate value in the "% Complete" column to indicate the work completed on each task. Alternatively, use the "Mark on Track" option in the Task Ribbon.
6. If a task is complete, update the "% Complete" as 100% and adjust the date in "Actual Finish" column.
7. "Reschedule the uncompleted works to start after": "Status Date" for the entire project. This option assigns constraint dates ("Start No Earlier Than") to tasks that were not completed as per the schedule and checks for changes in the project forecast dates.
8. If the forecast dates are within the contractual dates or baseline completion dates and are achievable, proceed for converting file into PDF. Otherwise, adjust the forecast dates by changing the relations to align with project goals and constraints.

Step 3: Evaluate Constraint Dates

1. In the Gantt Chart view, review the "Constrain Date" and "Constrain Type" columns for each task.
2. Identify the type of constraint applied to each task, such as Must Start On, Must Finish On, ASAP, ALAP, SNET, SNLT, FNET and FNLT.
3. Make note of the specific dates associated with the constraints, if applicable.

Step 4: Assess Impact of Constraint Dates

1. Evaluate the flexibility of the project schedule based on the constraint dates.
2. Identify any conflicts or clashes between tasks with fixed constraints and the project's critical path or dependencies.
3. Determine if the constraints need to be adjusted to accommodate changes or if they align with project goals.

Step 5: Analyze Schedule Deviations

1. Switch to the Gantt Chart view by clicking on the View tab and selecting Gantt Chart.
2. Identify critical tasks that directly impact the project's timeline and completion date.

3. Review the schedule for deviations, such as tasks that are behind schedule or have changed durations.
4. Identify slippages or delays in the project schedule.
5. Analyze how schedule deviations or delays affect subsequent tasks and the overall project timeline. If the slippage is impacting the project completion date and is justifiable, proceed for circulation with the team. Otherwise, prepare a mitigation plan.

Step 6: Adjust Schedule and Reschedule Tasks

1. Resolve conflicts by modifying or relaxing constraints, if possible, to alleviate clashes.
2. Use Microsoft Project's rescheduling capabilities to adjust task start and finish dates, and update dependencies as required.
3. Reevaluate the critical path after making adjustments to ensure an accurate representation of the project's progress and timeline.

Step 7: Communicate Updates and Report

1. Distribute the updated project schedule to relevant stakeholders, such as team members and management. If there are no comments from the rest of the team, circulate it with the client.
2. Generate reports using Microsoft Project to highlight schedule changes, critical path updates, and any potential impact on the overall project timeline.
3. Schedule meetings or discussions with stakeholders to address any concerns or questions arising from the schedule update.
4. Foster open communication and collaboration among team members to facilitate a shared understanding of the project's progress and any adjustments made.

Check List for Weekly Report Preparation

Sl. No	Description	Check box
1.	**Safety Shares:** **Check Points** Week safety topic needed to be mentioned. Any unsafe findings and the rectification needed to be mentioned. Weekly TBM or training Photos needed to be attached.	
2.	**Safety Shares** Manpower: Manpower shall be in average/max of people present in the week. Shift: shifts involved in the week (provided by HSE dept) Hours: Manhours involved in the week (provided by HSE dept) Other data related to DSTI, Plan task observation etc. will be provided by HSE dept same shall be maintained in the PPT **Check Points** Manpower, Shift, Hours, Other data related to DSTI, Plan task observation etc.	
3.	**Manpower Plan** Man power present in the week (average / Max of the week) shall be updated according to Expat and Locals separately. Total – Manpower (%) is the dividend of the cumulative of each Colum and **Check Points** Previous week and This week manpower shall be updated.	
4.	**Manpower Histogram** Graph shall be bar-chart, current month cumulative shall be updated in total actual manpower. Check for the changes in the bar-chart, current month bar chart needed to be updated automatically. **Check Points** Bar chart updated with current month cumulative	
5.	**Contractor HR / IR matters** **Check Points** Transport Food Manpower	
6.	**PPE Register-MSS overall Project PPE Record** PPE record will be updated by store team and same will be shared by HSE team for weekly update. Total received – Issued in the project = Overall stock **Check Points** PPE record updated	

Sl. No	Description	Check box
	Overall stock calculated	
7.	**Risk Assessment** Risk assessment will be assessed by the HSE team and same will be provided in the weekly report. **Check Points** Risk assessment provided.	
8.	**Method Statement Register** Method statements Register includes previously submitted, under approval, and under preparation statements. The QC team will prepare the method statements, which are updated on a weekly basis. **Check Points** Method Statement Register updated.	
9.	**QA/QC Data Book Tracker** Data Books are prepared by QA/QC Team and shame will be shared with Planning team on weekly basis. Document status Remarks are needed to be updated in the register. **Check Points** QA/QC Data Book Tracker updated.	
10.	**Test Book Tracker** Test Books are prepared by QA/QC Team and shame will be shared with Planning team on weekly basis. No of Test performed: Current week, till last week and Cumulative are updated on weekly basis Remarks are needed to be updated in the register. **Check Points** Test Book Tracker updated.	
11.	**Incident/Accident Register** Incidents/Accident of the past week will be recorded in the incident/ Accident Register. This register is needed to be prepared by HSE team and same will be shared to Planning Team on weekly basis. **Check Points** Test Book Tracker updated.	
12.	**Plant Ramp Up** Plant Ramp up plan in obtained from the Tender submission documents. Current month / Week Equipment utilization will be listed as actuals. Ramp up histogram is a bar chart consisting the plan Vs actual of all the months as per the Tender documents. Graph will be updates on the basis of the actuals of the current week. **Check Points** Plant ramp-up plan updated	
13.	**Plant Register** Plant Register consists of the Equipment with the respective model No, no of quantity, Driver, Nationality, Certificate, Licence, Medical Check, Safety Training, Training Date and Ready to work.	

PRACTICAL PLANNING ENGINEERING

Sl. No	Description	Check box
	This report shall be checked with HR department and HSE team. Updates shall be requested from HSE Dept and latest changes needed to be updated in the Weekly report. **Check Points** Plant Register checked	
14.	**Material Delivery** Material updates are sent by the Procurement Team on weekly basis. Every week there will a procurement related meeting and any delays shall be updated discussed. Planed dates and actual dates shall be compared and in by any case the difference in more then 2 weeks an early warning needed to be submitted via C.Com to client. **Check Points** Material tracking updates	
15.	**Project Progress S-Curve** Progress S-Curve is obtained from the Schedule. Upon changing the status date on weekly basis planned progress will vary, same shall be tabulated as a planned progress. Actual progress shall be updated on weekly basis and obtained actual progress will be tabulated against the planned progress against the date. Along with the actual progress a progress variance, forecast completion date shall also be updated. **Check Points** Planned Progress, Actual progress, forecast date and variance updated	
16.	**Commodity Chart** Commodity chart is a bar chart with the quantities planned in the week along with actual and total quantities that are tabulated. **Check Points** Quantities planned, actual, and total updated	
17.	**Schedule** Schedule is a programme given to client consisting timeline along with the progress percentage that needed to be updated on weekly basis. Follow the check list of the schedule update. Check List is prepared separately for the schedule update. **Check Point** Schedule updated.	
18.	**Progress Summary:** Progress summary shall consist of the progress achieved in the current week photos, planned and actual dates along with progress of the respective WBS and activities that will be performed in the next week along with the hindrance **Check Points:** Planned Date. Actual Dates. Photos. Planned progress, actual progress and variance.	

Sl. No	Description	Check box
	Quantities/commodities if client requested.	
19.	**Weekly Lookahead** Weekly lookahead is a lean board prepared for the work to be done in the current week and next week. Current week work done needed to be updated. Next week plan to be provided. **Check Point.** Weekly lookahead is updated.	
20.	**Challenges / Hindrance and Delays.** Hindrance found in this week shall be updated along with the last week in the register. This register shall also consist closing date and current status. **Check Point.** Register is updated.	
21.	**Early Warning Register.** Early Warning raised in the current week and along with previous early warning shall be listed here. **Check Point.** Register is updated.	
22.	**TQ Register.** TQ raised in the current week and along with previous TQ shall be listed here. **Check Point.** Register is updated.	
23.	**SI Register.** SI raised in the current week and along with previous SI shall be listed here. **Check Point.** Register is updated.	
24.	**NCR Register.** NCR received in the current week and along with previous NCR shall be listed here with the current status and the comments. **Check Point.** Register is updated.	

Working On MSP (Project Tracking on MSP)

Project Scope and Objectives:

- Clearly define the scope and objectives of the project.

- Identify the deliverables, milestones, and key activities.

- Break Down the Project into Tasks:

  Identify all the tasks required to complete the project

- To facilitate project management and task organization, it is essential to develop a Work Breakdown Structure (WBS) that breaks down the project into smaller, more manageable tasks.

- To ensure effective monitoring and evaluation, it is necessary to separate interface milestones from the Engineering, Procurement, and Construction (EPC) WBS. This segregation allows us to track interface activities independently from the overall project activities.

- Moreover, the WBS needs to be further subdivided into individual WBS elements based on materials during the Procurement phase. This breakdown enables efficient management of the procurement process, ensuring the timely delivery of required materials.

- Similarly, during the Construction phase, the WBS should be divided based on different areas. This division allows for proper resource allocation and progress monitoring in specific construction areas, optimizing the execution of construction activities and adhering to project timelines.

- To achieve a higher level of detail, the WBS should be further broken down into specific activities. This breakdown facilitates the assignment of responsibilities, estimation of resource requirements, and effective tracking of progress within the project.

- By implementing a comprehensive WBS, we can streamline project management, enhance coordination between teams, and successfully complete the project.

Determine Task Dependencies

- Identify the dependencies between tasks (e.g., Finish-to-Start, Start-to-Start, Finish-to-Finish and Start to Start).

- Define the logical sequence in which tasks need to be executed.

- Maintain the Total Slack i.e., ZERO, so that delay impact can be assessed effectively.

Estimate Task Durations: -

- Estimate the duration required to complete each task.

- Consider the availability of resources, dependencies, and any other factors that may impact task durations.

Assign Resources

  - Identify the resources (human, equipment, materials) required for each task.

- Assign resources to tasks based on availability, skills, and expertise

Load Resources

- Enter the resource assignments into the MSP schedule.

- Specify the amount of work each resource needs to perform on each task. (only if client is requesting the resource loaded schedule).

- If client is not requesting the resource loading, change the duration in to the work by multiplying the duration with 100 or 1000 (Higher the value more accurate the update will be) and load the obtained value as units in a task. We can also use the cost of each activity as the work units required to complete the activity.

- Please note the engineering shall be 5%, procurement 20%, and construction 75%; in any case, procurement shall not exceed 20% in order to maintain the greater weightage of construction because construction will have more activities than procurement.

- The cumulative of the total units shall be loaded in the "Max. Units" and the Type as "Work"

Define Task Constraints and Deadlines

- Set any task constraints or deadlines that need to be met.

- Specify any scheduling constraints that may effect the project timeline.

- There should not be constrains while updating the schedule as constraints will not allow the project to update. Hence maintain the lag in the relationship between the activities to obtain the desired dates.

- Activity Type shall be Fixed work, as this type of activities can be updated by varying the durations while updating the project, thus the overall weightage distribution will remain same as allotted.

Set Baseline

- Save a baseline of the schedule to track and compare against the actual progress later on.

- This will serve as a reference point for measuring project performance.

- After saving the baseline any change in work will not change the baseline work hence needed to re-baseline again to maintain the same weightage of the work.

- Note the work = Duration x Resource (Total manhours required for the completion of the activities)

- To compare the actual progress with planned progress formulas needed to be inserted in certain columns

- Number 1:

  - Custom attributes shall be Formula: [Baseline Work].
  - Calculation for task and group summary rows: Rollup – Sum.

- Number 2:

  - Custom attributes shall be Formula : IIf([Status Date]<[Baseline Start],0,IIf([Status Date]>=[Baseline Finish], 1, ProjDateDiff ([Baseline Start], [Status Date])/ProjDateDiff([Baseline Start], [Baseline Finish])))
  - Calculation for task and group summary rows: Use Formula.

- Number 3:

  - Custom attributes shall be Formula : [Number1]*[Number2]
  - Calculation for task and group summary rows: Rollup – Sum.

- Text1: Rename as Planned Progress %

  - Custom attributes shall be Formula : cInt(IIf([Baseline Work]=0 And [Number2]=1,100,IIf([Number3]=0,0,([Number3]/[Number1])*100))) & "%"
  - Calculation for task and group summary rows: Use Formula.
    - Note: Planned Progress % will work on the status date.

Track Progress and Update Schedule:

- Update the schedule on a regular basis to reflect real work progress.

- Use the % Work Completion column to update, and any change in update can impact the Work Variances thus monitor the work variances.

- Upon update of every activity project update for "reschedule uncompleted work to start after (Status Date)" for "entire project" needed to run.

- After each update work variance needed to checked if there is a variance between Baseline work and work, copy the work from the baseline work column i.e., row in which variance is and past in the adjacent Work cell.

- Compare the completed work, remaining work, and actual start and finish dates against the planned schedule.

Adjust the Schedule

- When updating the schedule, ensure that the actual start and actual finish dates do not contain any future dates than the status dates, and that there are no dates before the status date that do not have any update on the start date.

- If there are any deviations from the planned schedule, make necessary adjustments and readjust the relations to retain the completion dates.

- In any instance, if the project's completion deadlines have slipped, a mitigation strategy must be established in order to keep the completion date. Mitigation may necessitate the use of additional resources, so mitigation strategies must be assessed by project managers.

- Modify task durations, resource assignments, dependencies, or constraints as needed

Communicate Schedule Updates

- Share the updated schedule with relevant stakeholders.

- Communicate any changes, delays, or impacts to the project timeline.

Continuously Monitor and Control

- Monitor the progress of the project on an ongoing basis.

- Keep the schedule up-to-date and make regular updates

Project Cost Management

Importance of Cost Management —

- ➢ IT projects have a poor track record for meeting budget goals
- ➢ The CHAOS studies found the average cost overrun(the additional percentage or dollar amount by which actual costs exceed estimates) ranged from 180 percent in 1994 to 43 percent in 2010
- ➢ A 2011 Harvard Business Review study reported an average cost overrun of 27 percent. The most important finding was the discovery of many gigantic overages or "black swans".

What is Cost and Project Cost Management?

- ➢ Cost is a resource sacrificed or foregone to achieve a specific objective, or something given up in exchange
- ➢ Costs are usually measured in monetary units like dollars

- ➢ Project cost management includes the processes required to ensure that the project is completed within an approve budget

Basic Principles of Cost Management -

- ➢ Most members of an executive board better understand and are more interested in financial terms than IT/project terms , so IT project managers must speak their language
- ➢ Profits are revenues minus expenditures
- ➢ Profit margin is the ratio of revenues to profits

- ➢ Life cycle costing considers the total cost of ownership, or development plus support costs, for a project
- ➢ Cash flow analysis determines the estimated annual costs and benefits for a project and the resulting annual cash flow .

Monitoring and Controlling Projects -

- ➢ Monitoring and controlling of project work encompass a process of tracking, reviewing, and regulating the progress of a project to meet the performance objectives defined in the project management plan.
- ➢ Projects benefit only from a properly conceived and implemented project controls strategy.
- ➢ Controls are essential in managing projects to success. and if proper controls are in place and if the dynamics of the project escalation process are understood, project managers and executives can learn to avoid failure.
- ➢ Monitoring a project includes collecting, measuring, and distributing important information that is accomplished throughout the length of a project.

Monitoring and Controlling Projects Continued –

- ➢ The monitoring and controlling of a project are associated with the following:
- ➢ Comparing actual project factors such as scope, cost, schedule, resources, performance, and values against the project management plan
- ➢ Identifying new risks
- ➢ Analyzing, tracking, monitoring, and managing already identified risks as well as newly identified risks
- ➢ Making sure that appropriate risk mitigation plans are being executed

Monitoring and Controlling Projects Continued –

- ➢ Assessing project performance and implementing corrective and preventive actions as necessary
- ➢ Providing information to project plans using the inputs from project teams and other stakeholders
- ➢ Forecasting to update current costs, resource allocations, and schedules
- ➢ Monitoring implementation of approved changes as they occur .

Integrated change control –

- • Integrated change control focuses on identifying the factors that influence the proposed changes, evaluating such influences, and managing the changes in real time during project implementation.

- To accomplish integrated change control, the inputs are project management plan, work performance information, change requests, environmental factors, and organizational process assets.
- Work performance information is essential to the project management plan and includes the following:
- Progress of projects or status of projects
- Progress of project deliverables or status of project deliverables.
- Start status and completed status of project activities
- Budgeted costs versus actual incurred costs
- Resource utilization details.

Integrated change control continued -

- The integrated change control process includes reviewing all change requests, approving or denying changes, and controlling the approved changes throughout the project lifespan.
- The change management activities in a project are part of the integrated change control process.
- When a change request is received, the following steps must be accomplished:
- The requested change needs to be identified within the project.
- The factors that are affected by the change must be identified.

Benefits of Integrated change control –

Acknowledgment: First of all, we as "Planning Engineer" Team would like to thank all of our members who interacted and participated with us through this topic. This document was originally initiated by Planning Engineer website by creating a form to collect member's questions and answers that might face a planning engineer during the interview. Planning Engineer team reviewed questions and answers to remove duplicated ones, added more explanations and graphs to the answers, and produce the final product in a good shape. In this topic you will find the most common Questions and the Model Answers that you may expose to in your Interview for a Planning Engineer Position.

Question No.1: **What is a constraint in primavera?**

Ans -Constrains in primavera is to fix the early or late start or finish dates of an activity as per following options: A-Project Must Finish by B-Mandatory Start / Mandatory Finish C-Start / Finish On or After D-Start / Finish On or Before E-Start / Finish On F-Expected Finish.

2. **what is the clause to be refereed in FIDIC when there is entitled for extension of time .**

Clause 20.1, "If the Contractor considers himself to be entitled to any extension of the Time for Completion and/or any additional payment, under any Clause of these Conditions or otherwise in connection with the Contract, the Contractor shall give notice to the Engineer, describing the event or circumstance giving rise to the claim. The notice shall be given as soon as practicable, and not later than 28 days after the Contractor became aware, or should have become aware, of the event or circumstance".

PRACTICAL PLANNING ENGINEERING

3- Question No.3: What is the reasonable range of float you assume while checking the look ahead work activities?

The float range is varied from a project to another. However, in my opinion 10% of project duration is the maximum reasonable float for any project.

Question No.4: What is the Critical Path? How you identify it and if any activity having negative slack, how can you adjust the duration?

Ans - Critical path is usually the activities on the longest path with zero float. Any delay on these activities will lead to delay in project duration. Usually critical activities are shown in red color or say zero float in columns. For reducing duration, you can adjust it by reducing the duration or changing the relationship between activities. However, planning engineer should pay attention to maximum resources (resources constrains) while crashing the critical path. Negative slack is usually resulting from constrains in the activities. Planning Engineer should follow up the negative float path and find the wrong relationships or constrains and fix it.

Question No.5: What is the difference between Planning & Scheduling Engineer?

Ans - Planning Engineer can work along with the project team to develop a complete time schedule including cost of resources. Planning Engineer can lead the team and influence his/her point of view. Scheduling Engineer can only follow senior planning engineer or project manager instructions to create logic between project activities, but s/he can't develop the time schedule alone.

Question No.6: What is the difference between Retained Logic & Override Logic?

Retained Logic is Invariably that will produce the longest critical path but if activities have been progressed out of sequence, there could be some illogical dependencies remaining, in particular resulting from dependencies with duration. Progress override invariably produces a shorter critical path and again there could be some illogical lack of dependencies resulting from activities having been progressed out of sequence.

Question No.7: What is the difference between recovery schedule and revised schedule?

Recovery schedule keeps the same finish date with some corrective actions to recover the delay such as add more resources and break down some activities and so on... Revised schedule we have a new finish date because of claims or adding a new scope of work (amendment).

Question No.8: You are working on a project and somewhere in the middle of the project. The progress variance was -5% and still you are achieving the contractual completion date. How is it possible?

Contractor is working on critical path and delays are on non-critical activities .

Question No.9: How can you define the Critical Path in primavera?

Simply filter the activities with Zero Total Float

Question No.10: As a planning Engineer, "Walk me through a project":

This Project is "Project Name" and it has a budget of "Project Budget". The Project started in "Project Start Date" and planned to be finished in "Project planned finish date". According to the last update date on "updated date" this project is (ahead/behind) the schedule where the planned % = X and actual % = Y, therefore the forcast completion date is Z .

Question No.11: How can you differentiate total float and free float?

Total float represents the number of days that can be delayed without affecting the completion of the project, whereas free float determines the number of days that can be delayed without affecting the successor activity.

Question No.12: What is Resource levelling and What is Resource Allocation?

Resource levelling is the best scenario to execute the works with the available resources. In order to achieve the best scenario, planning engineer could change the activities durations and/or activities dates without affecting the project overall duration to maintain best usage of resources. While Resource allocation is assigning resources to activities, determine the amount of labor, equipment and money required for any activity.

Question No.13: If we increase 2 days to the duration of any activity on critical path that will increase the duration of project by 2 days?

Yes. It is on the critical path which means it as Zero Total Float and any increasing in its duration will affect the duration of project.

Question No.14: Explain what a good schedule means?

Scheduled activities must reflect the project's contract scope of work) b) Dates must be in accordance with contract. c) Meets the contractual requirements /milestones. d) Activity durations are reasonable: activity duration must be calculated based on quantity of work and resources available to be applied to the work.

Activity relationships are all defined, as review must be take place all relationships have been included and all are valid and redundancies are eliminated, and no open ended activities except the first and last activities. f) The critical path makes sense g) It considers procurement and material and equipment deliveries h) It must be cost and resource loaded I) Must be accessible in proper format, complete, clear, and convenient. j) Specific must tell about what will done, who will do, when will do, and what cost will need .

Question No.15: How will you make a manpower loading for your schedule?

 Manpower loading is based in my company productivity rates, we calculate the required man hors for each B.O.Q item by using this formula :
Required Man Hours = QTY / (Productivity Rate)

Question No.16:
What are the involvements of Project Planner and vital Role in Project Management?

Since Planning Engineer directly involve in project management activities, project leadership to make decisions concerning the development of plans, and how work process broken down & the control how it be managed. Track, review, forecast & give inputs the status of the Project and product. Further planning engineer should raise the flange to project team where s/he recognize and potential risks .

Question No.17:
Float belong to the Owner or the Contractor?

It is a question that you probably will not find a definite answer for.
The significance of the argument about who owns the float has two
folds, first its ability to directly or indirectly influence the construction
methodology and/or sequence once the project execution has started,
and secondly, the potential entitlement of extension of time (EOT) and the application of liquidated damages (LDs). There are mainly three
views of the matter which are presented hereinafter .
1. The 'contractor owns the float' argument -
This is the traditional view and still has its appeal among many practitioners. This view implies that the contractor is entitled to utilize float for his own risk events and recovery rescheduling.
Not so far ago, a survey in the United Kingdom suggested that 80% of the respondents assumed that the contractor owns the float; not surprisingly, the majority of those respondents were contractors .
2. The client owns the float argument
This is just the opposite of the view above, the proponents of this view
argue that the client has paid for the project and the program is one
of the tools to manage the project and monitor progress, therefore, the
client should be able to control the float to reduce costs and control
progress, especially when the program is a contractual requirement
in which the contractor has developed it for the client's benefit .
3. The 'project owns the float' argument
This view basically says float is owned by neither the contractor nor the
owner. The project owns the float which means "float is not for the
exclusive use of any of the parties and it serves whoever needs it first"
if it is used in good faith.

Question No.18:
What are the methods of calculating EV (earned value)?

1-Updating actual cost of activities
2-Updating the actual budgeted units of activities
3-Updating the actual resources comparing to budgeted ones

Question No.19:
What is the difference between recovery plan and revised plan?

Recovery plan is made with acceleration to remain within contractual completion date but revised plans accounts for change order which may or may not be within contractual dates .

Question No.20:

If the Project Total Float shows negative, does it always follow that the Performance % Complete is less than Schedule % Complete?

No. Performance % Complete has nothing to do with the network logic or the critical path. It is possible that certain activities with high budgeted value might have been progressed better than plan but other activities that has less value are the ones driving the critical path and delays the project completion date.

Question No.21:
How to calculate budget man-hours?

In order to calculate budget man-hour, you must have the budget quantity for each activity, from that and through the standard man-hour, convert the quantity into man-hours based on organization productivity rates, the total of these man-hours will be the budget man-hours.

Question No.22:
What do you mean by SDK , & what is its usage in Primavera?

Its stand for " Software Development Kit " it is used in Primavera to export quickly all the resources , cost etc. from Excel to Primavera. It is a powerful tool, but it has some limitations with Excel version, i.e should 32 not 64.

Question No.23:
How do you start planning without any information on hand?

Gather the necessary Materials, such as the Scope requirements, project start, and finish dates and any documents needed to produce project objective .

Question No.24:
What is redundant logic?

It means that if successor of A is linked to B and B is linked to C Also Successor of A linked to C then the link between A to C is called redundancy.

Question No.25:
Is Quality and Grade are same thing?

No, there is difference, Quality is the performance of the requirements and fitness to use, Grade is a matter of different technical characteristic.

Question No.26:
Define the main responsibilities of the planning engineer in each phase of the project's lifecycle. Please state clearly which information/data you would need from the Project Manager/Project management team in order to fulfill your task as a planner.

This question is tricky because it tests your understanding of the whole planning process throughout the project's different phases. Moreover, you should fully understand the specifications and legal documents related to the project in question. However, you will not find it difficult to answer this question if you have been involved in the responsibility of only one completed project from inception to hand over.

Question No.27:
What are the monitoring skills?

Ability to sort data, checking authenticity of data, Analyze and Predict data, Generate Reports.

Question No.28:
Could you chase Project Managers for information's and not just be a keyboard Junkie?

An answer for this question could be that I have developed very good interpersonal and communication skill which accords me the ability to politely yet consistently pull for the needed answers I require to get my own side of the job going and yet maintaining a healthy rapport within My team of busy PM's.

Question No.29:
What is the best software for planning?

No software for planning, it is only for scheduling, the planning process only done in brain. However, oracle primavera is the best planning tool that helps to create time schedules.

Question No.30:
What would you submit if your consultant / client asks you to submit a matrix report?

It is an incomplete request. I must know which matrix you need, resource matrix, cost matrix, authority's matrix, engineering/procurement matrix etc. else that would be a wide report containing more than 50 columns of P6.

Question No.31:
Mention 4 reasons cause -ve float in primavera:

Using project must finish by
o Using Constraints
o Using different calendar in one project
o Using relationships with other project

Question No.32:
What is the difference between Float and Slack?

There is no difference between float and Slack. It is two different words of same meaning.

Question No.33:
What is the difference between negative lag & lead?

There is no difference. It is two different words of same meaning.

Question No.34:
How do you explain project delay if earned value is more than planned value?

The contractor has performed better in areas which are not on longest path "The Critical Path". In another words, the contractor executed the right quantity in the wrong place.

Question No.35:
How are early and late dates determined?

Early Dates in a network is determined by Forward Calculations And late dates is determined by backward Calculations .

Question No.36:
What are three methods of measuring project progress?

Key Performance Indicators "KPI's", Cost Performance Index "CPI", Schedule Performance Index "SPI".

Question No.37:
What is the best way to be professional planning engineer?

Understand the project management concepts, tools, and techniques. -Practice doing real projects and get comments/review from expets. -Continuous improvement by learning new tools that would help to increase the accuracy of decrease the time required for tasks.

Question No.38:
What are SV and CV?

Schedule Variance (SV) & Cost Variance (CV) in Project Cost Management. Schedule Variance and Cost Variance are two important parameters in earned value management which help you analyze the project's progress. Schedule variance (SV) = Earned value (EV) – Planned value (PV) Cost variance (CV) = Earned value (EV) – Actual cost (AC) .

Question No.39:
What's the way to resolve the delay in project time?

Fast Track: Reduce activities duration, resequence, reschedule without affecting the project total duration, fast tracking has a problem regarding the quality issues if it is applied in a wrong way. Crashing: Reduces activities durations, resequence, reschule but with additional cost to achieve better results. this additional costs could be:
-Acceleration Costs to subcontractors.
-Bonus.
-Additional costs result from less productivity due to increasing the manpower in workplace.

Question No.40:
If Budgeted cost of works is more than actual cost of works, how do you consider the performance of Project? Optimum, Bad or Good?

Good. Since we are spending less money than planned, but we also need to check if we are on schedule or not.

Question No.41:
What is Project Management?

Project management is the application of processes, methods, knowledge, skills and experience to achieve the project objectives. General. A project is a unique, transient endeavor, undertaken to achieve planned objectives, which could be defined in terms of outputs, outcomes or benefits.

Question No.42:
What does it mean if "SPI" greater, lesser or equal to one?

SPI greater than one means ahead of schedule, less than one means behind the schedule & equal to one means as per schedule.

Question No.43:
Could we have more than one critical path?

Critical path is a dynamic path where it could be changed every time we update the schedule, change durations, or relationships. However, the critical path of a project is one path that could have too many activities underneath. Therefore, the project has only one criitical path.

Question No.44:
Scope is known partially, then how to plan for future?

Through the life of the project as more information is available more work to be planned called agile management. Accordingly, we can use agile management to plan the known part of the project only and keep the scope of work until we have more information about it.

Question No.45:
What is concurrent delay?

Concurrent delays have two meanings:
o When two events of delay on critical path are occurring at the same time, one affecting activities on Contractor's risk and the other affecting activities on Employer's risk.
o OR two or more events of delay on project critical path that belongs to one only of these parties contractor or client .

Question No.46:
What is a Baseline?

Baseline is the value or condition against which all future measurements will be compared. The baseline is a point of reference. In project management there are three baselines – schedule baseline, cost baseline and scope baseline.

Question No.47:
What is the Difference between Bar chart & Network Diagram?

Bar charts and network diagrams are used to display visually the complexities and dependencies of project work. Network diagrams display the project work as linkages through the chronological flow of work from start to finish. Gantt charts visually display primarily the work breakdown and the associated durations. Both charts graphically show work breakdowns, enabling managers and workers to easily identify conflicts, co-dependencies and determine the effect of change in the system .

Question No.48:
What is Thresholds in project Management?

It is the project management technique in which lower and upper values of a parameter are specified against which project data can be evaluated and monitored. It could be applied on WBS level as well as activity level.

Question No.49:
What is difference between crashing and fast tracking?

There are basically two techniques that can be used to shorten the project duration while maintaining the project scope. These techniques are fast tracking and crashing.
Crashing is the process of adding resources to one's project to be able to finish it faster. It has cost impact.
Fast Tracking, on the other hand, is the process of performing tasks in parallel to be able to finish the project sooner. It does not have any cost impact, but increases the risks.

Question No.50:
What is the normal productivity of welder for Carbon steel material per day?

This question is to test your knowledge of productivity rates. However, you shouldn't memorize all the answers in your mind, your answer could be "I don't memorize all productivity rates since it is vary from an organization to another and from worker nationality to another. However, i have some standards that I refer to when the organization productivity rate is not available.

Question No.51:
What is the difference between free float and total float?

Total float is the amount of time that an activity can be delayed without delaying the project completion date. On a critical path, the total float is zero.
Free float is the amount of time that an activity can be delayed without delaying the Early Start of its successor activity.

Question No.52:
For an activity, if the free float is negative whereas the total float is positive. Is this possible to happen and what's the impact?

It may happen depends on the activity flow, but that doesn't mean this free float will affect the completion of the project since the total float is positive.

Question No.53:
Define critical path:

A critical path is the sequence of project network activities which add up to the longest overall duration, regardless if that longest duration has float or not. This determines the shortest time possible to complete the project.

Question No.54:
Does primavera loads cash in and cash out in same schedule?

Primavera deals with cost of the project only (cash out) but you can work around with making a resource called cash in/out to view cash in/out .

Question No.55:
How to reduce critical path?

A- Compressing schedule by fast tracking, crashing, reduce scope, Cut quality.
B- Fast tracking: Results in rework, increase risk, requires more attention and communication.
C- Crashing: increase cost, increase management time
D- Reduce scope: negative impact on customer satisfaction
E- Cut quality: increase risk, requires good matrices.

Question No.56:
What is the normal total float allowed for a new project?

Total float should be not greater than 10% duration of the total project duration. (This percentage is subjective).

Question No.57:
What are the duties of a planner?

Assigned in overall/master schedule, look-ahead targets, and accomplishment reports and monitoring.

Question No.58:
What is Baseline Program?

An agreed Program that use to compare the actual result to measure performance of project or product against what was planned.

Question No.59:
What is SF dependency? Any example. Have you ever used this?

A logical relationship in which a successor activity cannot finish until a predecessor activity has started. Example: The first security guard shift (successor) cannot finish until the second security guard shift (predecessor) starts.
I don't think I have ever used this, but I have generally thought of a Start - Finish dependency as being used where an agree period of handover is required between two activities.

Question No.60:
Are all activities with negative total float drive the project completion date?

Not all negative float activities drive the project completion date. Only the chain of activities driven by their dates and logical relationship drive the completion date and it is called the longest path.

Question No.61:
What is meant by recovery schedule?

Recovery schedule is a revision of the Program's Master Schedule updated on a certain data date. The Engineer requested the Contractor the recovery schedule to show on how the contractor he'll be going to recover the incurred delays up to date.

Question No.62:
What do you mean by "EPC", "TIA" & "EOT"?

EPC stands for "Engineering, Procurement & Construction "
TIA = Time Impact analysis
EOT= Extension of Time

Question No.63:
How do you get information to populate and update your schedule?

Organize a planning workshop with all the Subject matter experts in attendance, plan all your questions needed for you to make up a plan and schedule. Extract all information from them, develop a high-level initial schedule and populate the WBS and activity lists. Later on planner should develop forms to be filled by project team in weekly basis.

Question No.64:
What is the standard deviation of the activity equal?

standard deviation for activity is = (Pessimistic duration - Optimistic duration)/6

Question No.65:
Suppose you have a conflict with the project consultant/ owner representative about a schedule update you have submitted recently. You believe that you have the right to reflect some time delays in the schedule in favor of your company, but the owner wouldn't accept that. The conflict escalated and the consultant hold the monthly payment till you agree on the update according to his perspective. He's also implicitly threatening to kick you out of the project unless you are "cooperative". What's should you do?

Unfortunately, this case is very common in the middle east. The power of consultant is over estimated, and engineers, especially juniors, will find themselves in similar situations in one way or another. My answer would be that you should communicate with your Project Manager immediately. It's not enough to have a casual conversation during the tea break; you should do that in "WRITTEN" format only. You should clearly explain the situation; why you think you have right in your claims; what would be the consequences in case you agree with the requirements of the consultant; and what are your concerns regarding the situation. In most of the cases, if the project manager is strong enough, he will exclude you from direct contact with the consultant till he solves the issue; and it might be necessary to consult the company's lawyer for assistance.

Question No.66:
What does it means If my free float is positive?

It means I can delay this activity without delaying the project end date.

Question No.67:
What to look for when a contractor sends their tender program to be awarded?

Tender schedule is summarized by natural. However, it should tell the contractor strategy of exciting the project and the project overall planning.

Question No.68:
What is an S–Curve?

S-curve is a graph showing cumulative cost or value (measured in terms of money or man-hours) against time.

Question No.69:
How De-watering works could affect your schedule?

That based on calculation of building own weight to be equal to or more the uplift force. Dewatering is required to reduce the uplift force of underground water. When this force is less than the weight of building, then dewatering activity could be finished. Planner should check with the project team when it is recommended to stop the dewatering and plan accordingly. Normally dewatering will hold the backfilling and external works around the building.

Question No.70:
Every project plan has two type of dates, the early start early finish and the late start late finish. Late start always starts after early start but finish with the early finish, Why?

Late start denotes the total float of the activities which allows the activities in the early stage of the project to get as late as possible while in the late time of the project there are mostly critical activities are left which does allow the late dates to pass over.

Question No.71:
What is the major difference between Cost variance and Schedule variance?

Schedule variance=Earned value-Planned value. It is related to the time or data date. Cost variance=Earned value-Actual cost.

Question No.72:
Why negative lag/lead is not recommended in a good schedule?

Because other relationship types can serve the same purpose. For example, instead of using FS relationship with negative lag, you can use SS relationship with positive lag.

Question No.73:
What does variance in s curve indicate on both axis?

Variance on Y-axis represents the value of (Money, ManHrs., etc.), while X-axis represents time variance .

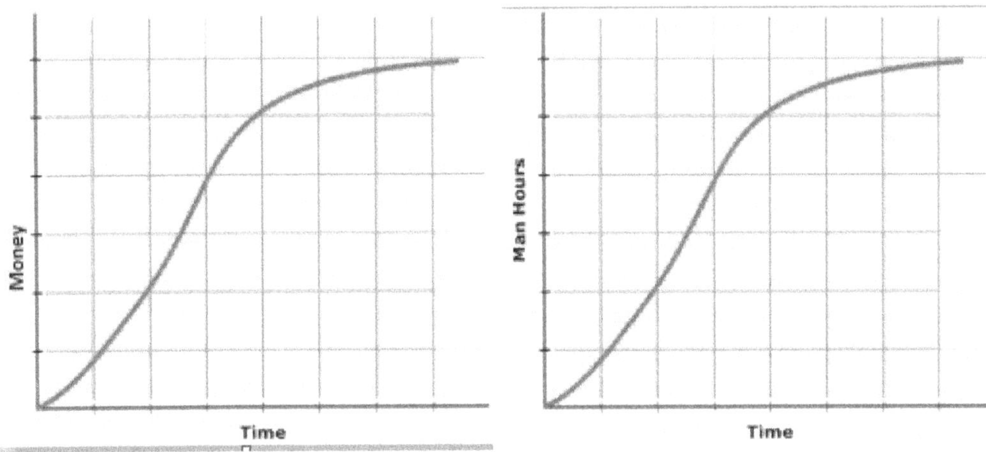

Question No.74:
What is an open end activity

An open ended activity is an activity that can end at the last day of the project without delaying the overall projects. An open end activity is normally not followed by any other activity and its completion can be delayed (within the project life) in order to focus on more important activities have successors (activities which can start only at the end of the earlier ones).

Question No.75:
If you are loading the cost in Primavera, Which cost will you select either in price in BOQ or your Budget amount or Both?

It depends, if this schedule is for the consultant, then the budget amount (selling price) should be loaded. However this is a case where the contractor would like to monitor the actual cost, in that case actual cost could be loaded. However, cost control is better in excel than primavera.

Question No.76:
What does trend analysis means?

A trend analysis is an aspect of technical analysis that tries to predict the future movement of a stock based on past data.

Question No.77:
A project shows actual performance is matching the planned performance. The Project is in delay also. What could be the reason?

The reason is, the progress is made on the non-critical activities than on the critical activities.

Question No.78:

What is the difference between flag and milestone activity in primavera?

Milestone & flags both are events rather than activities. Some client likes to use flags rather than milestone due the following differences.
1. With the use of flags the logic of main event can be easily tracked as these cannot be created without predecessor as standalone allocating the constraint. Whereas milestone can.
2. Flags cannot update manually as Primavera automatically update the status whereas milestone can be update manually.
3. Flags cannot be constraint only driven by predecessor whereas milestone can.

Question No.79:
How do you estimate activities durations?

By generating meetings & follow ups with contractors and other persons related to construction, this is also related to the contractual milestones. Normal activities can be estimated from experience. Special activities can be estimated by having meetings with project team and experts in this field. However, the project overall duration is the main constrain that might affect all other estimations.

Question No.80:
What does it mean if "CPI" greater, lesser or equal to one?

CPI greater than one means over budget, less than one means under budget & equal to one means same as per budget .

Question No.81:
What is needed for a successful project plan?

Contract document, drawings, B.O.Q as primary & other planning tools as secondary support. Furthermore, the involvement of project team in the planning, estimation, and sequence of work would result more accurate project plan.

Question No.82:
We hire the team in execution, then who planned for the project?

The planning of the project is made during the project life cycle with different level of details. For example, during the tender stage, the tender team is responsible for the high level of planning. However, when the project is awarded the project team is responsible for the planning and breakdown .

Question No.83:
How often you update your Project Baseline ?

It varies from project to project, depending on reporting/progressing periods. However, the working schedule should be updated on a continuous basis, as each activity is started or finished.

Question No.84:
What are BCWS, BCWP, and ACWP?

These three acronyms are earned value terms that stand for Budgeted Cost for Work Scheduled (planned value, or PV in the PMBOK Guide's in my opinion ill-advised neologisms), Budgeted Cost for Work Performed (earned value, or EV), and Actual Cost for Work Performed (actual cost, or AC.)
BCWS is what was budgeted for each work package as scheduled .
BCWP is the sum of the budgets of all completed activities/milestones.
ACWP is the sum of what it cost to complete each of the work packages/milestones .

Question No.85:
What is a constraint?

A limitation that reduces the efficiency with which a project can be accomplished.
Resource availability is a type of constraint that can delay a project's schedule and efficiency.
In general, constraints should not be input to the schedule until after the schedule has been optimized through critical path analysis.

Question No.86:
What is activity & What is WBS ?

Activity is a task or process to be accomplished in a set period as part of working toward a larger project goal. An Activity can be assigned to a resource(s) and have an associated cost. Activities are ordered with logic links
Work breakdown structure, a hierarchical format for identifying, displaying, reporting, and changing project work. Since the WBS is the "skeleton" of work on which the resource, cost, schedule information is draped, it is the principle tool for implementing scope/cost/schedule integration.

Question No.87:
What is a milestone? What are the types of milestone?

A milestone is an event. Activity-driven milestones are usually entered PM software as activities with durations of zero. Since milestones have no duration, once they are reached, they are immediately in the past. It is therefore good practice to name activities using the past participle of the verb (i.e., "Test component" = activity; "Component tested" = milestone.

Project Management Interview Questions and Answers

During the project management interview, you will be asked interview questions that focus on your training and experience with the successful delivery of different projects. You can also expect behavioral or competency-based questions that explore essential project manager skills such as team building and team management, planning and organizing, negotiation, problem-solving, leadership and adaptability. Let's start with the likely project management interview questions that explore your experience on project delivery.

1-Tell us about your experience in managing different projects and how this can contribute to our position.

It is important to structure your interview answer because this is a multi-layered and complex question. Start by explaining how you will answer the question. This keeps your answer on track and to the point. "I will begin by giving you a short description of my last three projects. I will then detail the skills and abilities I developed as a result of each project and then demonstrate the value of these skills to this position." You can then go on to provide a brief but concise summary of each project. "I was the project manager for the XYZ project and this involved ..." Then describe the skills you acquired during the project. "I encountered a number of difficulties on this project that required an innovative approach. I used group problem solving sessions as one of these approaches. This worked well because it helped each team member to clarify their particular project role and responsibility and we were able to develop plans and realistic schedules that the whole project team contributed to ..." Demonstrate how these skills will benefit the position and company. "Projects now are faced with tighter budgets and fewer resources. This approach maximizes the available resources and keeps everyone focused and motivated for the duration of the project..

2- Describe how you recently managed a diverse project team towards a common goal .

Focus on your ability to delegate in a fair and practical way, how you clearly defined project roles and responsibilities, kept personality clashes and conflict to a minimum and monitored and fed back to the project team. Outline your management style and why it worked.

3- Describe the most complex project you have managed from start to finish.

Provide a comprehensive answer remembering to explain the project as you would to a client and not to somebody who has been involved in the project. The more complex a project, the more formal processes and techniques are needed to effectively manage the work. Explain the purpose, value and implementation of the most critical aspects of the project including managing the project work plan, the project schedule, the project risks, the project issues and closing the project. Be enthusiastic about your accomplishments and specify how your experience will benefit the company. Point out where you made a difference on the project in terms of expenditure, quality, efficiency, customer satisfaction and business and organizational success.

4-What do you believe more in, a Leader or a Manager and why ?
This question is also more from agile mind-set where rather than managers, leaders are required and the team is self-organizing.
It's important to answer this question as honestly as possible because both the qualities are

required for multiple scenarios. Leadership is required for Project Management as without that a manager can't become a great mentor and role model for the team. At the same time, the manager is required to manage project efficiently and has to take some tough decisions during the course of the project.

Management .

5- How do you deal with underperforming project team members ?

If you are an experienced professional, you might have worked with a demotivated or underperforming colleague. The critical point for the project manager is, he or she has to motivate all project resources to produce the most out of their capacity. Project manager must motivate underperforming resources in a project.

This project manager interview question assesses your people management skills. This question will show how you motivate your underperforming resources.

6- What is Work Breakdown Structure (WBD) and how does it affect the work estimates of tasks/activities .

WBD is the process of decomposition of a project into deliverable-oriented components. This helps the project manager to oversee the project more effectively.

7- What are the techniques for doing "activity time" estimates ?

The techniques are parametric estimates, three point estimates and analogous estimates.

These are some of the popular questions that are asked in project management interviews. Always be prepared to answer all types of questions — technical skills, interpersonal, leadership or methodology. If you are someone who has recently started your career in project management, you can always get certified to understand the industry-related terminology, skills and methodologies.

8- Can you describe some of the projects that you handled in your previous job ?

They don't want the entire list. Pick some examples based on the following criteria:

How recently have you worked on it? (Don't talk about a project that happened years ago)

Has it been successful? (Don't talk about the one in which failed .

9-Describe all the steps involved from the time of project initiation to project completion ?

The best answer for this question would be scenario-based. Sometimes, the interviewers themselves give a hypothetical project and ask you how you would handle it.

For each stage phase the project follows, briefly mention the following:

The main objective of that phase
The key people involved
Your role in each of those phases

10- Did your colleagues or your manager ever challenge your decisions ?

Many people think that it's better to say 'no' to this question and move on to the next. But, disagreements in projects are quite common. So, it is extremely unlikely nobody disagreed with your decisions (Especially, if you are a senior project manager). So, it's better to say yes and go on to describe how you handled the situation. Show that you are a person who can take feedback constructively and can take everybody along with you in a collaborative manner.

11-What is a decision support system (DSS) ?

A DSS is used vastly in enterprise applications, mainly MIS & ERP based systems. It provides automation and stability in the decision-making process of the organization. There are two types of DSS, structured and unstructured. DSS connects many flow charts in the organizational process. It can be formulated and built statistically or stochastically.

12.How do you keep your team members motivated ?

One of the important roles of a leader is to keep the morale of the team members high. Show the interviewer that you are team player and work collaboratively. Tell the interviewer that you would like your team members to look up to you for advice. Also, they should feel free to share their ideas and suggestions with you. Instead of imposing decisions, you allow the team members to contribute and make it a collective effort.

13. Do you think integrity is an essential quality of a project manager ?

Of course, you have to say 'yes'. Go on to describe why it is so. Any company wants an employee who shares the values and principles of the company. If you are in a responsible position such as a project manager, you are expected to show the way for others to follow. Earning the respect of your team members and the trust of your bosses can only happen when you are ethically upright.

14-What is a Fish bone diagram and when to use it ?

Fishbone Diagram or Ishikawa Diagram is a visualization tool to understand potential causes of a problem to identify its root causes. It is used usually in brainstorming sessions so that the team's conversation is focused on the actual problem and not stray away towards only the symptoms.

15-Can you tell me an example of how you communicated a failure to your team, manager and customer ?

This project manager interview question will assess your risk management and communication management experience together. Bear in your mind that, failures, emergencies or critical points about a project must be communicated face to face. If face-to-face communication is not possible, then, you should choose teleconference meeting or phone call.

Project Manager Interview
Following can be a good sample answer for this project manager interview question.

We were working on an online learning portal project of an oil company. Deadline of the project was Feb 15, 2016. Although we completed our development tasks and internal tasks on time, customer could not complete their acceptance test on time.

Executive management of the customer was pushing to deliver the project on time. However, since customer could not complete their acceptance tests, it was risky.

First, I called my manager. I wish we could have spoken face-to-face but she was in a business trip at that time. I told her the situation. She agreed with me to speak about the risk of the situation with the customer.

Then, I organized a meeting with the project team. I told the team that they did all they have to do. I added in the meeting that, we, as project team, met our deadlines and objectives. However, customer could not complete their acceptance tests on time. Therefore, we will be postponing the project launch for one month. This made some of the project team members upset because we were working hard to complete the project on time, but the project was postponed because of a customer-sourced delay.

Finally, I organized a meeting with executive management of the customer. During the meeting, I told to the project sponsor and executive managers of the customer that, customer acceptance tests are not complete yet. In addition, if we launch the project, we might face critical problems on live environment, and this can cause dissatisfaction and lose of reputation. At the end of the meeting, executive managers were agreed to wait till customer acceptance tests completion.

This answer shows that the project manager approaches to the failure communication in a systematic way. First, he reports to his manager. If his manager would not accept the situation or propose alternative ways with the project team and customer, he could have changed the approach to the team and customer respectively.

After getting the approval of the manager, he speaks with the team first and then communicates to the customer respectively.

16. What is a project goal? What is its significance ?
Answer:
Every project when it needs to be accomplished is generally divided into small phases or modules. Now each of these modules can be considered as a goal. Accomplishing a goal means a specific module which

can be related to the development of a project has been completed. Thus, a number of goals need to be accomplished to meet the final outcome of a project.

17-All leaders have to deal with conflict situations. Describe a recent disagreement you personally had to handle ?

Answer:

Leadership interview questions that explore how you handle conflict are looking at your ability to understand and respect different views. Demonstrate your ability to settle disputes by focusing on solving the problem taking into consideration the personalities involved. Show how you evaluate the viability of the different dispute resolution mechanisms available and are able to provide support and expertise to other people. Demonstrate how you are able to negotiate a compromise.

18-What do you mean by Work Breakdown structure ?

Answer:

It is nothing but an approach in which a project is breakdown into the smaller modules. The primary aim is to pay equal attention to every aspect of a project. The team efforts can simply be enhanced with this and error-free outcomes can always be assured. It also makes sure of timely deliverables.

19- Is it necessary for tasks to be completed in a logical sequence ?

Answer:

This actually eliminates any form of confusion and at the same time, it makes sure of error elimination. It is actually not always necessary to accomplish them in a logical sequence. The tasks which are daunting can be first accomplished so that their impact on other tasks becomes clear. However, completing them in a sequence always make sure of favorable results.

20-What was the biggest or most challenging project you managed ?

Answer:

You have to be prepared for this project manager interview question. Because, your answer to this question will show your limits about your experience. Note that, this question might come with additional questions asking about how many people there were in the team, who you were reporting to, and how many projects in total you were managing at the same time.

Before sitting in your project manager interview session, go through your experience. Choose the most challenging project that you were involved.

The most challenging project I was involved was Golden Gate Bridge Construction Program. I was managing the project of construction of the towers that will carry the bridge. There were three architects, six civil engineers and 47 construction workers in my team. In total, I managed 56 project team members during this project. The most challenging part of the project was meeting the deadlines. Because, several other projects were dependent on my project. Any delay in my project was causing delays on the rest of the project. For instance, a one-day delay in my project was causing 200 hundred construction workers to wait for our work to be completed. And the cost of one-day delay was around $80,000. This was causing a big pressure in executive management of the company and therefore it was a big challenge for me as well.

First highlighted part in this answer shows the size of the project team that this project manager managed. Second highlighted part stresses the challenge of the project financially. Provide numbers, budgets and statistics if you have any. These will make your answers stronger.

21. What values do you think a project manager should have ?
Answer:
Everybody has their own idea of values. However,, it should focus on the job profile and associated with project management.

22- What was the biggest challenge that you faced while working on a project ?
Answer:
'I didn't have the right team'. 'I don't deal well with changes. 'My boss wasn't very supportive'. These would be bad answers to give your future employer. As a project manager, you are expected to manage people and handle risks. So, don't tell your interviewer that you fall short in those two areas. Give an example of a situation in which the challenge was due to the external factors. It can be about when the project was abruptly shelved or when the funding for it has been stopped. Don't forget to mention how you handled the situation and what you learned from it.

23- What is most challenging aspect about being a project manager ?
Answer:
While you can answer this question based on your understanding and past experiences, make sure that while answering this question you do not demonstrate your inability to deal with some of the most critical aspect of project management. Challenges can be empowering, so try to structure your answer around this.

24-What would you say is the most important skill of a Project Manager and why ?
Answer:
A Project Manager is responsible for planning and executing projects. Whilst they may not be working directly on the specific activities that create the end-result, they work alongside the team to ensure that everything runs smoothly, on-time and the pre-agreed deliverables are met. They are also the first point of contact for any issues. This means that a Project Manager needs to master certain key skills, such as communication, teamwork and organization.

When preparing for upcoming project management interview questions, consider what you think is the most important skill and how you have demonstrated it in your career. You could also think about what the business you're applying for is looking towards. Did they give any clues in the job description perhaps? Circle back to the original job ad if you have to.

25-How do you monitor and review the delegated responsibilities ?
Answer:
This is an extension of the question on how you ensure that your team members meet deadlines. Talk about clearly defining the responsibilities, arranging regular meetings, empowering the team members to approach if there is any concern and constant updates on the progress of the work.

26-What is your work style?

Answer:

It is another question to check if you fit in with the company's culture. It also indicates whether you are self-aware to communicate your work style. Though it sounds vague, this question provides an opportunity to show how you can be an asset to the company. You could talk about your emphasis on speed and efficiency, how you like to work collaboratively, your way of communication etc. Further, you can mention about how you organize your day and how many hours you work.

27-How do you improve your knowledge regarding project management ?

Answer:

Companies want their employees to be fully invested in the jobs that they are applying for. There are many software tools coming up and many processes being invented regularly in the project management landscape. Hence, project managers need to continually upgrade their skills to be relevant. Basically, tell your interviewer about what you are doing to grow in your field. It could be certification courses you are taking or workshops/courses you are attending. Also, you can talk about your interactions with project managers and people in the field to stay up to date with the latest.

28-What is Effort Management in a project ?

Answer:

All the activities related to work in a project are measured by the efforts. It can also be defined as the proper allocation of time for resources to accomplish any task assigned to them. Communication, focus, motivation as well as self-discipline are the important factors to pay attention to. At the same time, it is necessary to record activities and pay attention to scheduling.

29-Did you face any problems with your co-workers in your previous company ?

Answer:

You might or you might not have faced issues with your former colleagues. But, if you mention that you did, don't be too negative. You can discuss the problem. However, put your emphasis on what you did to resolve the problem. Give it a happy ending. You can also talk about what has been the learning and how you would handle similar kind of people in the future. It shows your leadership skills.

30-How good are your communication skills ?

Answer:

Project managers need to have good communication skills. So, don't be too honest and say that communication skills are your weakest area. The answer has to either 'good' or 'excellent'. But, don't sound overconfident while saying so. If they ask for examples, be ready with two or three examples in different settings to justify your point.

31-What could be the key challenges that can declare their presence while managing a project ?

Answer:

Project Management is a vast duty and needs a lot of experience to closely monitor things and to pay attention to the same. A single error in the development can lead to the failure of an entire project. This can even impose a strict upper limit on all its functionality. In addition to this, some projects require integration of core languages which creates a lot of issues. Next big factor is the need of advanced skills to manage their sub-modules. Also, project management includes the use of right skills at the right time.

32-What is Lean Management ?
Answer:
It aims to impose a limit on the wastage of time and efforts during a project development. It makes sure that the development doesn't face any issue due to any factor such as unavailability of resources, server downtime and so on.

33-Do you have any questions ?
Answer:
Most of the applicants will say 'no' to this answer. But, by asking questions you can stand out from the crowd. It also shows your interest in the company. Your questions can indicate that you want to know a little more about the job you applied for. Or, you can ask them some questions about the organization itself.

A project management interview need not be dreaded. The above sample project management interview questions and answers should help you face the interviewer confidently. However, there can't be a single right answer for any of the questions. Use the answers as guiding tools but make sure you take into consideration your own experiences, background, strengths, and weaknesses while answering the PM interview questions. Good luck with your job hunt .

33-What is CMMI ?
Answer:
CMMI stands for Capability Maturity Model Integration. It is a process improvement approach that provides organizations with the essential elements for effective process improvement.

34-What is Six Sigma and how is it important in project management ?
Answer:
Six Sigma is a measure of quality that strives for near perfection. It is data-driven approach and methodology for eliminating defects. In order to achieve Six Sigma, a process must not produce more than 3.4 defects per million opportunities. If applied effectively, six sigma can approach can help finish a project on time, be reducing the risk of effects/failure.

35-Can you name the different modules of a project ?
Answer:
The very first one is the blueprint or deciding the design/features aspect of a project. Once finalized, it goes to the development phase where a team of developers lead by a technical lead pays special attention to its core development. Once deigns it is tested to check if there is an issue with it or not. This assures its functionality. Once tested, it might be used in beta version and finally the full version is handed over to the concerned department.

36-How you will define project management ?

Answer:

It is actually the discipline or the conjunction of planning, initiating, controlling, as well as executing a teamwork so that most desired outcomes can be achieved. As every project is different from the previous on handled by any organization in most of the cases, there is always a need to pay special attention to the concerned activities to make the project unique and best in every aspect.

37-How do you deal with changes to your project ?

Answer:

Changes and modifications are a part and parcel of most projects. An employer wants a project manager who is flexible and adaptable to changes. The best answer can be about how you actually put in place a change management process even before the changes occur. At the same time, showcase that you are not a person shy to say 'no' when you feel that a certain change is not suitable for the project

38-What is a project scope statement ?

Answer:

It defines the scope of a project along with other useful information at the same time. It is basically developed when a project is in its initial phase. One the primary aim is to make the other modules simpler and clear. A strong scope statement can also encourage the development and other teams engaged in a project to accomplish their assigned tasks in the best possible manner.

39-What are the factors that you will pay attention to about the resources while selecting your team ?

Answer:

Everyone in the team should be disciplined and co-ordinate with each other. Next factor is the right skills required for the timely development of a project. The experience of the team members plays a significant role in it. Selecting the team members that has specialization in that particular field can always lead to most favorable results for sure. Therefore, paying attention to it would be good.

40-Why do you want to work with this company ?

Answer:

You need to go prepared for this interview question. If their working style suits yours, you can discuss it. If the job you are applying for is the next logical step for your current job, tell them that. Or, even something like you being attracted to their work culture or vision, can be a good response. Better yet, you can say how the job and the company align with your personal growth. This shows that you are looking for a long-term collaboration with the company.

41-What defines the role of a good project manager ?

Answer:

The very first thing is obviously the Leadership quality following by right attitude. A Project Manager is responsible for handling all the activities and modules related to a project. The manager should have advanced skills to help the team to avoid any problem, conflicts, and other issues. In addition to this, a project manager always motivates the team to get the best out of them.

42-Can you name a few modules of Planning in a Project Management ?

Answer:

The very first thing is to get the formal approval to start the task. Next is to pay attention on the budget development. After this the next module could be developing the schedule followed by paying attention to the quality assurances. It is also necessary to estimate the number of resources required and if there is a need to have some special resources. Finally, emphasis is to be made on Risk Planning.

provide a lot of useful information for the next project to b developed.

43-What are the objectives of monitoring and controlling ?

Answer:

1. Keeping a close eye on all the activities related to a project
2. Keeping a close eye on the project variables
3. Risk Management and addressing the efforts that went wrong due to any reason.

44-What are "Severity Levels" in a project ?

Answer:

In any project, problems can be of different levels and it is not always necessary that they can be addressed with similar efforts. There is always a need to understand the right strategies to eliminate them. For this purpose, they are assigned different levels based on their complexity and the efforts required for solving them. These levels are:

1. High
2. Medium
3. Low
4. Trivial

45-Do you believe in team development? Can you share instances where you did that for your teams ?

Answer:

Team development and team management skill along with mentoring and leadership for the success of project is very important for good project management. This question is to understand if you believe in that.

In this answer, you need to express the people management skills you have developed with few examples. You need to showcase your leadership, mentoring, conflict management as well team grooming skills.

46-What do you understand by the Pareto (also known as 80/20 rule) principle/analysis?

Answer: It is a decision-making technique through which by doing 20% of the work you produce 80% of the desired result.

46-What is RAID in project management and why is it necessary to create a RAID log ?

Answer:

RAID is an acronym for Risk, Assumptions, Issues and Dependencies. A RAID log is   important for a project manager to track anything that would impact a project now or in the future.

47-Name the ten key knowledge areas as mentioned in the PMBOK guide ?

Integration Management, Scope Management, Time Management, Cost Management, Quality Management, Human Resource Management, Communications Management, Risk Management, Procurement Management, and Stakeholder Management.

48-Do you have international project team management experience ?

If the company you applied for is a multinational company, international project team management will be a critical evaluation factor. You might not have this experience. In this case, say no honestly.

This question might be followed by additional questions asking about how the experience was and whether you have any strange story about your international project team management experience.

Following can be a good answer for this project manager interview question.

I have managed a team of 15 project team members from five different nations. We were working in a natural gas implementation project in Brazil. There were natural gas engineers, environmental engineers and civil engineers in the project team. Five members were from Brazil, three members were from UK, three members were from Spain, two members were from India and two members were from Qatar. It was a great experience to learn from different cultures when working with them.

It was the first time for me to work with project resources coming from a Muslim country, Qatar. While most of the project team members were having Monday syndrome, engineers from Qatar were performing better than other project team members on Mondays! After some time, I asked these engineers why they are more willing to work on Mondays. I learnt that, their official weekends are on Friday and Saturday. Therefore, Sunday is their first weekday. Therefore, they were performing better on Mondays in our project since it is 2nd day of their workweek. It was a strange experience for me to see people better motivated on Mondays.

Project manager candidate answers the question with numbers through a real project he managed. Besides, he gives a strange experience he faced with his international project team management experience.

49. Describe one of the most challenging projects you've managed and explain what you learnt from the experience ?

Answer:
When it comes to challenging project management interview questions, make sure you prepare for this interview question. Don't simply pick the first example that comes to mind. Take some time to consider a few of the most challenging projects you've worked on and which ones you learnt the most from. An interviewer is interested mostly in seeing how you dealt with a situation and how you turned a negative into a positive, and ensured the project ended as a success.

These are just some project management interview questions that you could be asked at your next job interview. While this isn't an exhaustive list of questions, it's certainly a good starting point for your interview preparation.

50-What is project delivery ?

Answer:
When the project is completed, it is simply transferred to the organization for the clients it is built for. The time of delivery of different projects is different and varies depending on a lot of features.

51. Why did you choose PMP Certification ?

Answer:
It demonstrates your knowledge and dedication to constantly and successfully be a project manager. It's worth probing the skills of applicants. Find out the last project they handled with creative thinking.

52. What do you mean by project documentation ?

Answer:
It is a detailed report prepared before the execution of anything else or in the initial stage of development process.

53. What are some of the projects that you handled in the previous job ?

Answer:
As an experienced professional, you are bound to have a portfolio, and this is the right time to share such a portfolio with the interviewer. Make sure that the portfolio you share is authentic as your previous portfolio will decide whether the interviewer will be interested in you or not.

54. What can be the objective of project according to you ?

Answer:
It's nothing but to come with an outcome which best meets the expectation of one and all and is unique in its own ways. It must reflect the objectives of the client for which it is developed for.

55. What factors project management objectives can affect and how ?

Answer:
The biggest impact can be on the budget. It is quite true that the budget can be enhanced up to a great extent of the objectives are not paid attention on properly. Optimizing and allocating are the prime factors to consider at the same time as they can also be impacted by the project management

objectives. In addition to this, the biggest factor that project management objectives can affect is decision making.

What kinds of projects interest you the most? Why ?
Answer:
The one word that you need to focus on for this pm interview question is 'relevance'. Do your research about the company and the role you are applying for. Your answer for this should be about the kind of projects that the company can offer.

57. What is your current salary and compensation package ?
Answer:
Be honest when you are responding to this question. Note that, human resources departments of companies are very aware of industry salary benchmarks. Therefore, they will be able to estimate your salary and compensation package.

If you say a salary that is too much above the benchmark, you can even lose the job opportunity. Because, there will be a limit of what the company can pay for this position.

Briefly, tell what you earn and compensation package, when this question is asked in your project manager interview.

58. What is your salary expectation ?
Answer:
This is one of the last questions that you will be asked in your project manager interview session. There is not a concrete answer for this question. However, the common practice is, aim to increase your salary at least 20% in your next job.

Considering your current salary and compensation package, you should tell your expectations. You should not say a salary and compensation expectation that is too much above your current package.

59. When did you run into a serious conflict and how you dealt it ?
Answer:
This gives an idea of how well you do your job. Having a strong focus and finding a solution to each problem means a great leader. Project manager does this all the time, so make good relationship with people and don't rule them before knowing anything about them.

60. How do you resolve conflicts in your projects ?
Answer:
Conflicts are inevitable in a project. A good project manager must be able to resolve conflicts without hampering the motivation and relationship in the project team. By its nature, conflicts seem to be resolved in favor of one side over another. However, with good communication and conflict resolution skills, you can resolve the conflicts in a win-win situation.

This project manager interview question assesses your conflict resolution and communication management skills.

Following can be a good sample answer for this question.

I experienced several conflicts arising in my projects during my career. First thing to look when a conflict arises is the source of conflict. Conflicts can be between two project team members, between the team member and his lead, between two stakeholders etc. After knowing the source of conflict, I look at the alternative solutions to resolve the conflict. The best option to resolve a conflict is collaborating where all parties are happy. Of course, I try to find a win-win situation first. If this is not possible, then, I try to analyze the pros and cons of different alternatives for resolving the conflict. I try to demonstrate the pros and cons of each resolution alternative analytically because numbers, figures, statistics and mathematical approach is the best way to convince people for a solution. After showing the alternative solutions, I guide people to rethink about the conflict. I expect them to reach a consensus. If this is not possible again, I try to solve the conflict with democracy. For instance, if the cause of the conflict is a how to solve a technical issue in a software project, I show the options to the project team and expect the software developers to vote for the best option to resolve the conflict.

Project manager candidate approaches to solve the conflict in a win-win situation. Then, he approaches to demonstrate different alternatives in a mathematical approach. This is great. Because, if you can describe a solution mathematically with statistics, numbers, figures etc. you will eliminate most of the arguments about the topic. Then, he opens the conflict to voting. By this way, he ensures that the majority will decide what will be the solution. He is not forcing or directing on what needs to be done in the project.

61. What are the three words that describes you best ?
Answer:
This is actually a cliché interview question generally asked by human resources personnel. This shows hints about your personality and how your colleagues think about you in work environment.

When answering this project manager interview question, try to remember your positive attitudes and what your colleagues say about your work behavior.

62. When I am working on a project or task, I always keep in mind that "what is the expected result?" ?
Answer:
Sometimes, if you forget what you are trying to achieve, you can deviate from your targets. Therefore, keeping in mind the expected results help me to focus on what needs to be done during the project.

I try to rationalize status, progress and alternative solutions to a problem. I do this by approaching analytically to a problem. For instance, I create dashboards for waiting issues, waiting time, assignee etc in a project to monitor how well the project team is resolving issues. Similarly, I record the number of codes each developer produces a day to forecast remaining activities in the project.

Project manager candidate answers the three words that describe him best first. Then, he gives examples and justifications for each word.

63. Which one skill does a project manager need to succeed ?
Answer:
This question forces the candidates to decide one of the scores of skills needed of a project manager. This explains the experience and focus towards a project manager. Your greatest strength as a project manager should be your answer to this question.

Performance Evaluation

Performance Evaluation					Date:
Sl.No.	**Requirements**	**Weightage**		**Remarks**	**Sign**
1	Signed copy of "Scope of Work document" to available at site	1%			
2	Understanding Scope & Battery limits	1%			
3	Hardcopy of Approved Budgets available at site	1%			
4	Collect & Maintain all Tender Reference Documents required for Proper Project Execution	1%			
5	Follow-Up Engineering Deliverables on a regular Basis.	5%			
6	Maintain Hardcopy of latest approved Drawings at site	2%			

7	Raise Indents immediately after the drawings are finalized.	5%			
8	Develop Project Schedule (with the help of Planners) and Implement the same.	5%			
9	Follow-Up Indents on a regular Basis.	10%			
10	Follow-with Finance team for vendor Payments	5%			
11	Monthly Resource Planning (Manpower, Material, Equipment etc.....) for Cash Flow submission	5%			
12	Daily, Weekly Reports to management (Highlight Constraints, Delays etc..)	3%			
13	Generate & Follow Weekly Lookahead Plans With respect to available Work fronts & Resources.	3%			
14	Conduct Weekly Progress Review meetings (Highlighting Delays Constraints, Delays, Import material Status etc....)	6%			
15	Allocate Work to the team at least One day in advance, and track Productivity	5%			
16	Organize HSE & Quality Training for all Project Manpower	4%			

17	Implement Approved Method Statements & SOP's	10%			
18	Display HSE & QA / QC Posters at Job Site	1%			
19	Maintain Hardcopy records of Approved HSE Risk Assessment	1%			
20	Maintain Hardcopy records of Tool box talks	1%			
21	Maintain Hardcopy records of HSE Permits	1%			
22	Implement Proper House Keeping at site.	3%			
23	Attendance Reporting on a daily Basis	2%			
24	Maintain Material Inward outward records.	2%			
25	Review Budget Vs Actual Expenditure from Finance Team and take corrective actions where ever required.	2%			
26	Intimate Finance team for raising Invoice as per contract terms & Work Progress. Ensure Time to Time flow-up for payments.	5%			

27	Leadership Qualities	5%			
28	Execution Skills	5%			
Total		100%			

Construction Claims -:

1. Construction Claims

What is Construction Claims?

A construction claim is the assertion of a right demanding either additional time or/and payment due to the result of an action. It is possible to meet construction claims in all construction projects.

Why do Construction Claims occur?

Clients, contractors, and subcontractors of this environment try to reach their own goals and expectations in order to increase their benefits. Conflicts may arise as a result of this diversified goals and expectations of parties.

They can be originated by several other reasons such as inadequate project planning, changes in scope, change orders, errors and omissions.

What is the consequence?

If the conflicts are not managed successfully, disputes which affect the successful completion of the construction project may arise.

Claim Management

Claim management is an unavoidable process in construction project management which requires effective management practices during the entire life cycle of a project.

A typical claim management process basically has 4 phases as follows:

- Claim Prevention: The claim prevention process is activated at the Pre-tender and Contract Formulation phases of a project. Contract documents project plans and scope of work should include all requirements related to the project because after the award of contract the opportunity to prevent claim comes to an end.

- Claim Mitigation: Construction activities are generally performed in highly sensitive and outdoor environments. It is better to minimize the possibilities of occurring claim all through the progression of the contract. A well-defined scope, responsibilities and risks will help to decrease the possibility of occurrence of claims. Also, risk management plans play important roles in the phase of claim mitigation.

- Pursuing Claims (Claim Identification and Quantification): Claim identification can be done by analyzing both the scope of work and the provisions of the contract. Inputs of the claim identification process are the scope of work, contract terms, definition of extra work and definition of extra time requested. Once an activity is identified as a claim, it will be quantified in terms of an additional payment or a time extension to the contract completion or other milestone dates. In this phase, a schedule and critical path analysis should be made in order to calculate the delay of the project. In addition to that, additional direct and indirect costs originated from the claimed activity should be calculated.

- Claim Resolution: Claim resolution is a step by step process to resolve the claim issues. If an

agreement between the parties is reached, then the claim is resolved and becomes a change order. If the agreement is not reached, depending on the resolution terms of the contract the claim may proceed to negotiation, mediation, arbitration, and litigation before it is completely resolved.

2.   Characters of a Highly Impacted Project

A lot of projects are out of control and headed for claims and disputes. The characters of these projects are described as follows:

- The contractor bids on incomplete design documents;

- The contract is awarded to the lowest bid contractor but not necessarily the most qualified;

- The owner/engineer issues a large number of design changes;

- The owner is inadequately staffed to process the multitude of change orders and respond in a timely manner to the numerous RFI from the contractor;

- The contractor fails to prepare an adequate as-planned or baseline schedule to identify the planned sequence and duration of work;

- The contractor fails to maintain an accurate and updated progress schedule including identification of changes and cause of delays;

- The contractor requests a time extension that is denied because of inadequate support to recognize excusable delays;

- The project is completed late, the owner has paid a significantly higher price for many changes, the contractor now has a big delay and impact claim, and the owner withholds payments to cover its liquidated damages

3.   Effect on the Project

Large value claims may destroy the viability of a project or make construction more difficult by adding to the disappointment between the owner and contractor. If a sizable claim is found to be valid, an owner faces serious problems. New financing may be required, later occupancy may be necessary, income from operation of the facility or rent from commercial property may be delayed or lost, and staffs may have to be funded longer than planned to administer the project.

Most owners include contingency funds in their project budgets to cover the cost of claims. However, the contingency funds are usually limited and seldom are large enough to handle claims. If a project experiences unfunded cost increases, emergency actions may be required, such as a temporary halt to construction, requesting special appropriations, financing by additional borrowing.

Almost any of these solutions create serious problems for the owner, as well as the contractor, because lost time costs money. Nonreceipt of payments resulting from incurred costs not envisioned in the contract price may result in the contractor's financial capability becoming dangerously unstable, and his being unable to pay his subcontractors or suppliers. Subcontractors, in turn, may default and the project may collapse due to a lack of resources and money.

4. Situations Causing High-cost Claims

From Contractor:

- **Inadequate site investigation before bidding:** Too often, the contractor will bid work without performing an adequate site investigation into areas such as availability of qualified labor, labor productivity, weather patterns, underground conditions, and other competing projects in the area that would compete for the available labor. As a result of not doing their homework adequately, contractors
may then take every opportunity to prepare change order requests or file claims to make up for their bid errors.

- **Bidding below costs and over optimism:** this practice would be considered a deliberate underbid, presumably justified to break into a new geographic market or new line of work. After the excitement of winning the job disappears and the reality of losing big money on the project occurs, contractors may be persuaded to seek every opportunity to submit requests for change orders or file claims.

- **Slow mobilization**: Many contractors do not perform sufficient planning in advance to effectively mobilize for the project. After contract award, the owner informs the contractor that the site is available and ready for mobilization to begin. In a design-build or EPC contract, the start of construction is often optimistically planned to occur earlier than when the approved for construction drawings are actually completed, and equipment and materials are procured and delivered. Also, contractors may not move on to a site in an efficient or timely manner because of insufficient planning regarding the equipment and labor needs that are required.

- **Poor planning and use of wrong equipment:** the means and methods contemplated by the contractor's estimators to achieve the productivities anticipated by their bids are often not implemented in the field because inadequate planning is performed prior to mobilizing to the site. When lower than anticipated productivities are experienced, contractors will be on extra alert to identify claim opportunities.

- **Inadequate cost and schedule control systems:** these problems are associated with imperfect management planning and control. Possible explanations for why estimated costs for project activities are so inaccurate when compared to actual costs, and why planned schedules experience significant delay, include poor definition of work activities and improper control of schedules.

- **Performing defective work:** Owners may need to withhold progress payments from contractors that have performed defective work. The delay to the project completion caused by the time required to correct these defects may also justify the owner's liquidated damages claims.

From Owner -:

- **Inadequate and ambiguous scope definition in the bid documents:** a project's scope must be defined in enough detail for comprehensive scheduling, estimating, and resource allocation to be reasonably accomplished. Whenever the owner is unwilling to make a concerted effort to define the construction project in the early stages, problems will undoubtedly occur throughout the entire project life cycle.

- **Inadequate time provided for bid preparation:** Owners are always under economic pressures to start and complete a new project or a modification to an existing facility. As a result of these pressures, owners may rapidly prepare incomplete bid packages and then request fixed price or unit price bids by a date that does not provide the contractor with an adequate time period to investigate the site conditions, thoroughly read and understand the owner's specifications, verify the accuracy of the owner's quantities, secure quotations for equipment and materials, prepare an adequate project schedule, and estimate its costs for performing the work. When this occurs, the contractor can either choose to add significant contingencies to its estimate to cover the risks and hope that its bid is still within the owner's budget, or bid competitively in spite of the risks and hope that if it wins the bid, it can recover any unanticipated costs through change orders and/or claims.

- **Competitive bidding:** competitive bidding is the procurement practice in which the contractor, who leaves the most money out of his estimate (usually as contingencies), gets the job. The lowest bidder is also the one faced with the highest danger of loss if contingencies, i.e., risks, are encountered. They will search ways to cut losses by seeking additional funds through changes. While competitive bidding is often a sound procurement practice, the owner must recognize that a bid that is significantly below the other bidders is a claim waiting to happen.

- **Major changes in the plans and specifications during construction:** the owner is ultimately responsible for defining the scope of a project during the conceptual phase of the project; the scope will probably change quite frequently. However, changes that occur during the construction phase or even detailed design phase inevitably make life difficult for the construction contractor. Scope changes result from a number of situations, such as owner preferences, design reviews, constructability issues, safety requirements, hazardous operations reviews, and operations and maintenance concerns.

Unrealistic schedules and underestimated costs: Whenever time schedules and/or project costs are based on optimistic predictions of labor productivity, availability of skilled labor, good weather, quantities based on an incomplete design, etc., the project will be burdened with missed milestone dates, cost overruns, and even low morale among project personnel. Sufficient time must be allocated in the planning stage of a project to accurately estimate time and cost requirements.

- **Owner-furnished materials:** owners typically want to procure and furnish their own equipment for unique projects, such as power plants, chemical plants and refineries, because of favorable purchasing agreements with vendors or the special needs associated with such projects. Most owners fail to understand that contractors have specific materials management plans for the project – a plan for when that material will be installed and where it's going to be stored once it arrives at the site. Most owners have the mistaken belief that whenever owner-supplied material arrives on the site, the contractor can efficiently store or install the materials. The sequence of delivery of bulk material items such as structural steel, large bore piping, and piping supports is extremely important to the contractor's efficiency. Owners and contractors must thoroughly coordinate and schedule the delivery of these items. Contractors usually have installation schedules that they plan to follow, and this type of misunderstanding leads to significant material management problems.

- **Failure to give adequate and timely access to the work site:** when an owner does not provide the contractor with adequate access to the work site to complete its work in the timeframe and in unobstructed conditions that were anticipated in its bid, the contractor may file a delay and loss of productivity claim for the increased costs resulting from the access problems.

- **Delayed approval of submissions, shop drawings or materials:** these types of delays can often affect activities on the critical path of the project schedule and cause delay claims. The contract should state the turnaround time that is available to the owner to perform these tasks. In addition, the contractor should always state in its transmittals the date when it needs a response.

- **Unclear definition of Mechanical Completion**: owners typically designate the Mechanical Completion Date as the key completion milestone in the contract. When these dates have occurred, the owner can begin to start-up the facility. Also, this date is usually the date from which liquidated damages are measured. Final Completion is the last milestone before the contractor can completely demobilize.

- the contractor is merely completing punch list work or certain miscellaneous work that was not necessary for Mechanical Completion. Disputes often occur at the end of the project if the definition of Mechanical Completion is unclear. The contractor knows what it has to do for Final Completion, but

- each owner's requirement for Mechanical Completion may be different. For example, are as-built drawings and operating manuals required for Mechanical Completion? If the owner requires these items before it will agree to the contractor's declaration of Mechanical Completion, but the contractor was planning to submit these after it declared Mechanical Completion, a dispute may occur over liquidated damages.

5.   Reasons for Forensic Schedule Analysis

Forensic schedule analysis may include a prospective or forward-looking method which uses the contemporaneous schedules to forecast the impact from a current or future event. It may also include a retrospective or backward-looking method which uses the as-built schedule. The reasons for performing a forensic schedule analysis can be numerous and often concern the following issues:

- Relief from liquidated damages;

- Justification for a time extension;

- Proof of delay mitigation;

- Change Order impact to the critical path;

- Proof of concurrent delay versus "pacing";

- Demonstration of schedule acceleration (i.e., Time Impact Analysis results compared to as-built schedule)

- Recovery of compensable delay.

6.   Claim Entitlement Identification

Entitlement is the legal basis of the claim. It may be derived from the language of the contract

(for example, the Changes Clause). A thorough understanding of construction contract entitlement is a mandatory prerequisite to the identification of issues on a project that give rise to a contractor's

recovery of increased time and cost of performance. This understanding is also necessary for the analysis and preparation of a claim .

A few typical claim entitlements are listed **below**:

- **Delays:** problems beyond the control and without the fault or negligence of the contractor that prevent the contractor from proceeding with any part of the work.

- **Disruption:** any change in the method of performance or planned work sequence, contemplated by the contractor at the time the job was bid, that prevents the contractor from actually performing its work in that manner.

- **Directed Change:** the owner enjoys the right to make any change that generally falls within the scope of the contract.

- **Acts of God/Adverse Weather:** typically good for a time extension only if the conditions vary substantially from the norm.

- **Differing Site Conditions:** two types: (1) subsurface or hidden physical conditions at the site differing materially from those indicated in the contract; and (2) unknown conditions at the site of an unusual nature.

- **Acceleration:** performance of the contract work in a time period shorter than that originally contemplated by the contract or performing on time when the contractor is entitled to a time extension for performance.

- **Defective and Deficient Contract Documents:** if the contractor is bound to build according to plans and specifications prepared by the owner, the contractor will not be responsible for the consequences of defects in the plans and specifications.

- **Owner-furnished Items:** the owner's failure to furnish items in accordance with the contract.

- **Variation in Quantities:** the importance to the contractor is whether its unit prices are sufficient to cover its overhead and other costs if the number of units significantly changes from the owner's estimated quantities used to prepare the contractor's bid.

  Strikes: typically good only for a time extension

- **Suspension:** the owner's directive that work be stopped on a part or the whole of the contract.

- **Termination:** <u>two types:</u> (1) termination for convenience resulting from factors outside the contract; and (2) termination for default when a contractor's performance is not acceptable.

On a heavily disrupted project. one or a combination of several of the above entitlements may provide to the contractor the contractual basis for compensation for the increased cost of the work or extended duration of performance.

7. Establishing The Cause-Effect Link

A contractor's claim request must clearly identify what actions or inactions by the owner caused the compensable liability and which of the entitlements bear a direct relationship to the financial loss or schedule impact. This establishes the important cause-effect link that is necessary to support a construction claim, as shown in the figure below.

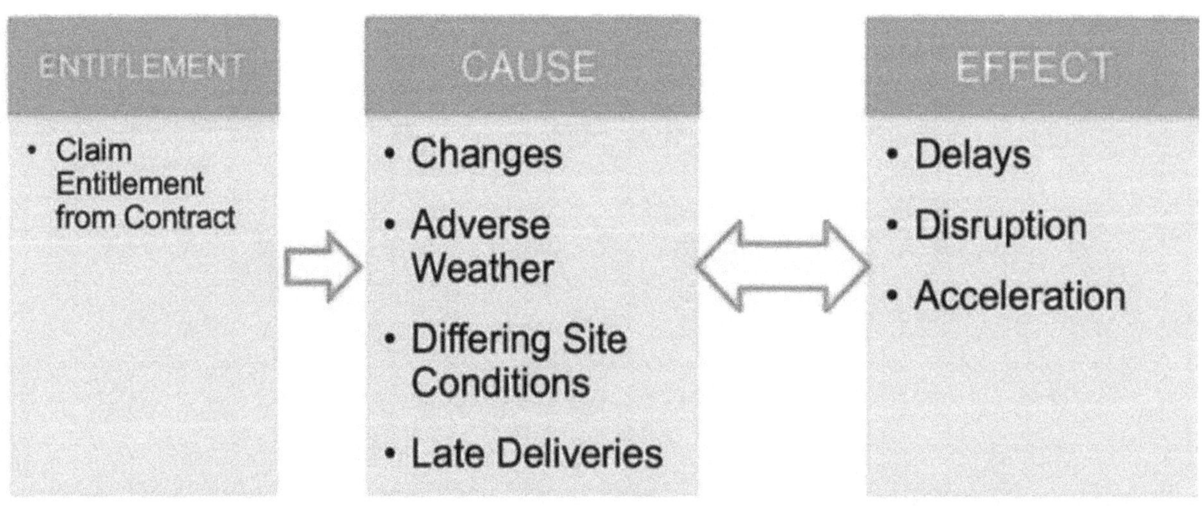

If the contractor does not comply with the stipulated requirements in the contract, a contractor's claim may be rendered invalid and rejected due to lack of contract compliance. All contractor claims must be supported by contemporaneous project records and documentation. More

specifically, the crucial element of proof needed for delay claims should be based on the contemporaneous project schedules used to execute the work.

8. Assessment of Schedule Quality

The underlying foundation for developing a supportable forensic schedule analysis depends on the quality and reasonableness of the project schedules. Checking the integrity of project schedule for obvious deficiencies is vital to ensure that the schedule is accurate and reasonable. If significant deficiencies exist, then the schedule used to measure, allocate, and assign critical path slippage could be flawed, and any resulting conclusions regarding the schedule analysis could be rendered unreliable Some vital schedule issues to evaluate include the following:

- Determine if the schedule complies with the contract documents;

- Ensure that the original contract scope and approved change orders are accurately reflected in the schedule;

- Check schedule integrity; and

- Compare schedule updates to the baseline schedule to identify significant changes.

8.1. Schedule Complies with Contract Documents

- An essential starting point is a thorough review and understanding of the contract documents. It is important to fully understand what documents and drawings are included and how they work together to define the scope of work. The various terms and conditions that define the contract administration procedures, notice requirements, responsibilities, and other contractual duties should be considered.

- More specifically, the contract documents will likely define, limit, or at least influence the direction of a schedule delay analyst and the selection of the appropriate schedule analysis method.

- Other contract clauses and requirements that need consideration regarding schedule delay are

  summarized as follows:

- liquidated Damages

- Time Extension

- Changes

- Mechanical Completion / Substantial Completion

- Weather

- Timely Notice

- No Damages for Delay

- Inspection of Site Conditions

- Differing Site Conditions

8.2. Original Contract Scope and Approved Changed Order

- An important quality check is to ensure that the complete original scope is represented in the project schedule. On large and complex projects, it is not unusual to find some of the original contract scope to be missing and accidentally excluded from the baseline schedule. This is especially the case when a rolling wave schedule development technique is utilized by the contractor. Therefore, it is important to verify to the extent possible that all required contract scope is represented in the baseline schedule. This is done by going through a verification process of the contract documents and other available project information to determine that the schedule accurately reflects the contractual Scope of Work. Areas for review may include the **following:**

- Engineering, including owner approvals of drawings and specifications;

- Procurement, including equipment and material delivery

- durations and customs clearance activities;

  - Construction, including the necessary detail to ascertain if all work is included and the critical path is realistic;

  - Pre-Commissioning activities

  - Start-Up and Commissioning activities; and

  - Quality assurance and quality control activities.

Omission of a required portion of the original work scope within the project schedule could produce a project schedule with an overly optimistic duration for the work because the full scope is not reflected in the schedule. As a result, forecasted early and late dates, float values, completion dates, and the calculated critical path may be unreliable.

In addition, if approved change order work is required to be incorporated into the project schedules, existing activity durations may need to be adjusted or fragnet activities may also need to be added to represent approved change order work in the schedule.

8.3. Schedule Integrity

Because the project schedule is a key management tool for measuring project progress over time, the project schedule should accurately reflect the impacts on specific works, milestones, and completion date. However, it is not unusual for the project schedule to be deficient because activity logic is missing, contractual milestones are artificially constrained, and actual dates are incorrect.

If a multitude of errors and deficiencies in the underlying schedule data exist, then the legitimacy of the schedule analysis may be invalid. Moreover, problems associated with the accuracy of project schedules may mask the true driving impacts that caused schedule delays. Therefore, the basis for claims may be in question. It is important to evaluate the quality and reasonableness of project schedules and identify potential areas of deficiencies that affect schedule accuracy. Common items that can negatively affect the quality of a schedule include the following:

- Excessive number of open-end activities;
- Overly long activity durations;

- Activities with excessively high float values;
- Conflicting as-built dates;

- Overuse of negative lags;

- Excessively long positive lags;

- Excessively long negative lags;

- Overuse of constraints; and

- Activities with incorrect status.

Without fixing these problems, the allocation of delay

responsibility may be entirely wrong. In the following paragraphs,

some of these deficiencies are examine

Excessive number of open-end activities:

- Open-end activities are defined as activities that have no predecessor,
  no successor, or both. In theory, all activities should have at least one
  predecessor and one successor except for:

    (1) the project start activity (no predecessor activity);

    (2) project completion activity (no successor activity).
- At a minimum, good scheduling practice should have a very small number
  or no activities with open-ends. A large number of open-end activities will
  create erroneous float within the schedule (in Primavera P6, the project start
  or finish date will be used to calculate the total float of open-end activities).
  Correcting open-end activities will change float values that may affect the
  critical activities.

Activities with excessively high float values:

- Float is defined as the amount of available time that the start or finish of an activity can be delayed without impacting a project's overall finish date.

- Schedule paths with high float values typically arise due to artificially constrained activities or other very long parallel critical paths. High float values can also result from a large number of activities with open-ends, which is a major issue.

- Schedules with a large number of high float activities should be examined and corrected for open- ends or missing logic links that would better optimize the planned dates of activities with high float values .

Inconsistent Use of Schedule Calculation Modes:

- Retained logic is often the default calculation mode that contractors typically use for calculation of the schedule. Another type of scheduling calculation mode is progress override. Progress override is typically used to accelerate a schedule which allows out-of-sequence work activities to progress without delay and not wait until its logical predecessor is complete.

- In many cases, contractors will use progress override as a way to update a schedule without having to spend the time correcting out-of-sequence work activities. If no reasonable explanation by the contractor is provided, then the inconsistent switching of schedule calculation modes between updates is a deficiency.

- A consistent use of schedule calculation mode as represented by the baseline schedule should be used for the schedule updates.

Overuse of Constraints:

- Constraints are defined as restrictions on either the start or finish of an activity.

- A large number of constraints should be avoided. Constraints artificially lock down a schedule and prevent a schedule to naturally "flow" during a forward and backward pass calculation to determine activity float values and the critical path of the project.

- The use of a constraint that affect or alter the critical path should be avoided.

- Constraints are also too often used as a shortcut tactic by schedulers when they do not have enough time to properly update the schedule or account for out-of-sequence activities.

Compare Schedules To Identify Significant Changes

- Popular delay analysis methods often employ some form of windows analysis approach, or schedule just before the delay event occur (e.g. TIA). These methods require the accuracy of contemporaneous schedule updates. Therefore, it is important to compare the schedule updates to the baseline, and between the schedules updates to identify changes made. Important schedule comparison checks include the following:

- Added and Deleted Activities;

- Activity Duration Changes;

- Changes to Activity Scope/Names;

- Changes to the Critical Paths;

- Changes to the Schedule Logic

- Added Constraints.

HOW TO
DEMONSTRATE
ENTITLEMENT

TO

Prolongation
Cost Claim

Summary of Contractor's Evaluation of Damages

1- <u>Extended Field Overhead</u>

ITE M	VALUE/ Month	ITEM	VALUE /Month
Superintendent	---	Site Truck & Fuel	---
Secretary/timekeeper (labor burden incl)	---	Consumables	---
Telephone (service & long distance)	---	Tools and Equipment	---
Fax (rental, paper, long-distance)	---	Subsistence	---
Couriers	---	Travel Time	---
Sundry Trucking	---	Bonds	---
Temporary Power	---	Insurance	---
Temporary Toilets	---	Extended Warranty	---
Office Building & Supplies	---		
Total Cost per month	A		
Total Month No.		B (from delay analysis)	
Total Cost (*Ax B months*)		A* B	
(---%) Office Overhead			
SUB-TOTAL		---	
Profit (---%)		---	
TOTAL		---	

- **Hints to assume the O.H**
  - **Extra Work field O/H.**
  - **Home Office O/H & Profit.**
    - In Principle, there is nothing wrong with claiming home office O/H and profit on its field O/H.
    - The % should be based on the mark-ups defined in the contract.
      - - each individual item
      - - within the charge out rates used to calculate labour impact
      - - as a separate component at the end of the claim
      - - under the guise of lost revenue
    - Substantiation Should be Requested.
    - Time Related Costs.
    - Consumables and Tools.
  - **Extended Warranty Period**

2- **Extended Equipment**

Item	value	notes
Equipment type)	-----	The value is (the delayed period * cost of the monthly rate)

  - This is an extended overhead cost and as such, the above amount should be substantiated.

3- <u>Overtime Premiums (acceleration cost)</u>

- Contractor contends that it accelerated the work with the knowledge of the owner who should pay for the cost.
- The owner contends that whereas it was aware that an acceleration program was ongoing, it was not aware that it was to the owner's account. It assumed the contractor was making good its own delays.
- A review of the records is required before deciding conclusively.
- It should have acquired a change order, as apparently occurred for other acceleration efforts. In this case, it is likely that the Contractor's silence will be his undoing.
- It is quite surprising how often one sees an acceleration program discussed in detail at the site with neither party seeking to ascertain who is paying for the program and how inefficiency costs are going to be addressed.

4- <u>Productivity Loss</u>

item	value	notes
Hours Expended (includes subcontractors)	-----	
Hours Estimated at Bid	-----	**<u>Justification required</u>**
Cost of the differences	----	

5- <u>Material Handling</u>

Additional equipment costs arising from downtime and standby time equal

- This is an extended field overhead cost and as such, the above amount should be substantiated.
- The lack of detail raises a number of questions, such as potential duplication.

6- <u>Safety</u>

Additional toolbox meetings and indoctrination downtime.

- o Contractor is arguing that because of the extended duration, it has experienced additional downtime.

7- <u>Delayed-Release of the Works guarantee</u>

item	value	notes
Contract Value	-----	
(---%) Works guarantee	A	
Interest at --% for the delayed period	----	% as per Contract

8- <u>Inclement Weather</u>

item	value	notes

This might be a valid claim subject to the following qualifications:

- ## the amounts need to be substantiated.
    - there has to be a demonstration that the delays being claimed did push the work into winter.
    - one has to ensure that no duplication exists with the costs claimed for extended duration and impact.

9- Disputed Extras

Justified extras refused by consultant

- Depending on the contract there may be some potential entitlement problems. One should ascertain if the contractor has satisfied the requirement to provide the appropriate Notice of Dispute.

10 **Labor and Material Escalation**
- If the project is extended, the contractor can be pushed into a period of higher wage rates or simply expend more labor in the period of higher wages. The same of course can apply to the material.

11 **Loss of Revenue**
- The revenue guaranteed towards the support of his home office will be reduced (if not eliminated) when a contractor encounters compensable delays.
- Home office costs are real and unavoidable.
- Home office costs (in the majority of cases at least) include: -
    - Estimation for projects to be tendered.
    - Accounting for the job and the corporation.

- - Purchasing.
    - Management of the overall direction of the corporation and frequentlyfor individual projects.
  - Head Office, per se, does not generate revenue.
  - No construction project could function without the head office.
  - Revenue for a construction organization is earned on the field.
  - Project bids must include an allowance towards the support of HomeOffice functions. Usually as a % of estimated project costs.
  - This allowance will yield the required contribution to allow the head office to function.
  - Eichleay Formula - most commonly used by contractors to
  - calculate loss of revenue.

Eichleay Formula

Step 1: $\dfrac{Contract\ Billing}{Total\ Billing}$ X Total Overhead = Overhead Allocatable to the Contract

Step 2: $\dfrac{Allocatable\ Overhead}{Actual\ Contract\ Duration}$ = Allocatable Overhead Per Day

Step 3: Daily Overhead X Delay Days = **Loss of Revenue**

12 Head Office Overhead & Profit

Utilities

Building

Computers

Administration

Management

Financing

Insurance

Bonding

Extended

Warranty Business

Development

The mark-up used in pricing this item should be equivalent to the mark-up allowance in the contract for extra work = (**X** %).

- Administration

- Purchasing

- Engineering

- Tendering

- Financing
- **Claim Preparation**

Based on the costs expended, claim preparation costs are (Y)% of the total claim: -

- The amount and method of calculation are quite difficult to accept.

- It is usually considered part of doing business.

- It should be noted, however, that if the dispute enters the arena of arbitration or litigation the costs of experts are considered valid compensable costs.

Manpower Productivity -:

Labor Productivity:

Brick Work - 1 mason + 1Labour = 1.25 cm

Wall Plastering - 1 mason +1 Labour = 10 Sqm

Ceiling Plastering - 1 mason + 1Labour = 8 Sqm

External Plastering - 1 mason + 1 Labour = 8 Sqm

Carpenter - 1 Skilled + 1 Un skilled = 4 Sqm

Bar bender - 1 Skilled + 1 Un skilled = 200 Kg

Tile work - 1 Mason + 1Labour = 10 Sqm

Painter - Skilled -OBD 600 Sft

Emulsion 800 Sft

CO-EFFICIENT FOR PAINTING:

Partly panelled and glazed doors = 0.80 times the door or window area.

Collapsible gates = 1.50

Corrugated sheeted steel doors = 1.25

Rolling shutters = 1.10

Expanded metal hard drawn steel = 1.00

Fencing and gates, brace, rails = 1.00

Flush doors = 1.20

Partly panelled doors = 1.00

Fully glazed doors = 0.80

Fully louvered = 1.80

 If its only for slab ,then a 5" slab almost costs roughly Rs.220/- per sq. Feet all inclusive of Steel, Rcc, Shuttering etc.

If u are asking for residential building complete in all respects…than it costs u around Rs. 1200/- per sq. Feet. Civil Structure Work – Rs. 750 per sqft and for Finishing Work – Rs. 450 per sqft.

(a) Painting - Rs 12 - 17 per sqft (two layers of putty + two layers of coat) including taxes

(b) Flooring - Marble is Rs 80 per sqft (depends on the type of marble may be - but this is what it is costing us). Granite and bathroom tiles 15 - 20 Rs per sqft (we provide all material such as cement, sand etc).

(c) Electrical - You are better off buying the materials for them. A rough guide is Rs 50 - 100 per sqft for materials and Rs 12 - 20 per sqft for labor.

CEMENT REQUIREMENTS:

M10 : 210 Kg

M20 : 320 Kg

M25 : 340 Kg

M30 : 380 Kg

M35 : 410 Kg

M40 : 430 Kg

M45 : 450 Kg

Thumb rule for concrete work

The concrete ingredients will be vary based on the mix ratio,

For Example,

If the Plinth area is 100 Sq.ft (10 x 10) and the required concrete volume is 100 x 0.04 = 4 Cum with M5 mix ratio means

Now from the below table which is for 1 m3

Required Concrete ingredients for 4 m3 of M5 is

Cement – 2.77 x 4 = 11.08 bags

Sand – 0.48 x 4 = 1.92 cum

Coarse aggregate = 0.96 x 4 = 3.84 cum

Thumb Rule of Concrete material requirement

Grade	Ratio	Cement in Bags	Sand in Cum	Coarse Aggregates in Cum
M5	01:05:10	2.77	0.48	0.96
M7.5	01:04:08	3.41	0.047	0.95
M10	01:03:06	4.44	0.46	0.92
M15	01:02:04	6.34	0.44	0.88

| M20 | 01:05.5 | 8.06 | 0.42 | 0.84 |
| M25 | 01:01:02 | 11.09 | 0.39 | 0.77 |

Thumb rule for Plastering Work

For plastering, the material quantity will vary based on the different mix ratio like concrete and the thumb rule for plastering work has listed below.

Type of Plastering	Mix ratio	Thickness in mm	Cement Bags/Sqm	Sand Cum/Sqm
Inner Plastering	1:3	15	0.16	0.017
External Plastering	1:4	20	0.17	0.024
Rough Plastering	1:5	16	0.11	0.020
Ceiling Plastering	1:2	12	0.17	

Thumb rule for Brick Work

The size of brick 190mm x 90mm x 90mm

Number of bricks per cum = 500 Nos

Must read: How to calculate the number of bricks

Mix Ratio and brickwork thickness	Mortar Thickness in mm	Cement in Bags	Sand in Cum
1:6 200mm Thk	10	1.4 / Cum	0.3
1:5 200mm Thk	10	1.7 / Cum	0.25
1:4 100mm Thk	10	0.15 / Sqm	0.035
1:5 200mm Thk Block 10 0.15 / Cum	0.02		